I0006609

A Study in E-Commerce Human Centered Technologies Design

A Study in E-Commerce Human Centered Technologies Design

Dr. Ralph T. Reilly

Writers Club Press
San Jose New York Lincoln Shanghai

A Study in E-Commerce Human Centered Technologies Design
All Rights Reserved © 2001 by Dr. Ralph T. Reilly

No part of this book may be reproduced or transmitted in any form or by any means, graphic, electronic, or mechanical, including photocopying, recording, taping, or by any information storage retrieval system, without the permission in writing from the publisher.

Writers Club Press
an imprint of iUniverse.com, Inc.

For information address:
iUniverse.com, Inc.
5220 S 16th, Ste. 200
Lincoln, NE 68512
www.iuniverse.com

ISBN: 0-595-18020-5

Printed in the United States of America

To my father

Foreword

This book is designed for Management Information Systems professors who choose to include the cognitive implications of human factors within interface design and how they play an important part in both sensation and perception.

A cross disciplinary text with MIS to include Ergonomist, Cognitive Engineers, Computer Animators, Human Factors Psychologists and Human Factors Engineers. Designed to be either the primary introductory human factors text or a supplemental text to be used within almost any area of study within computer aided design. Those areas would include hueristic evaluations, usability testing, human factors in decision making, statistical and experimental modeling, graphical user interface, prototyping, user-centered design, industrial engineering and pattern recognition.

With the explosion of E-commerce there are many interface design books, specifically for web applications that just do not include the human factors element in their design theory. This book is different than most because it uses actual experimental data to determine the importance associated with human factors and design.

The most important feature of this book is how human-computer interface is explained, through the use of "faces". The topic of faces as a universal icon lends itself for discussion by both the technical and non-technical audience alike. The information can be presented statistically, experimentally or graphically.

Preface

This research addresses three issues in facial processing: First, is gender significant in reaction to facial affect? Second, does a distractor play a role in the processing of facial expression? Third, how can understanding of the results of such a study contribute to the information systems implications involved in such a study? The research is an attempt to understand these questions while studying whether automatic, or preattentive, processing plays a part in the identification of the facial expressions.

Experiments Ia and Ib provided evidence that females processed faces more quickly than did males. Additionally, happy faces were processed more quickly than angry faces.

Experiment II was designed specifically to eliminate the distractor in an effort to determine if the distractor played any role in the processing time of the target faces. While the male subjects did not show any difference in test results with or without the distractor, regardless of target gender, test results for female subjects showed a marked difference in that there is evidence to support the hypothesis that females were, in fact, distracted in the distractor tests.

Thanks to that annoying kid who
stopped by to do the cutting and pasting.

Introduction

Facial Information Science is becoming a discipline in its own right, attracting not only computer scientists, but graphic animators and psychologists, all of whom require knowledge to understand how people make and interpret facial expressions. Computer advancements enhance the ability of researchers to study facial expression. Digitized computer displayed faces can now be used in studies. Future advancements will facilitate not only the researcher's ability to accurately display information, but to record the subject's reaction automatically.

Business uses of facial animation could include a more cost effective means of video telephony. Sending a television image of a person over the phone now requires a special high capacity phone line where the image must be transmitted 30 times a second. Instead, an image of the caller's face could be transmitted once, followed by programming instructions that automatically animate the computerized face. To the person at the other end, it would appear like a television image.

Artificial faces need not be confined to the screen. Professors at the Science University of Tokyo have created a mechanical face that can express emotions like anger and surprise, the first step toward development of human-like robots.

In the future people will communicate with a face on the computer display screen. Already, advancements in artificial intelligence allow humans to "communicate" with computers through voice pattern recognition. Future work in artificial intelligence will allow the computer and user to "read" each other's facial expressions, understanding what can be communicated through facial mechanics. Toward this end, significant research has been conducted since Darwin in an attempt to discover whether the processing of nonverbal facial emotion in humans is a preattentive or an attentive task.

Additionally, research in facial emotion processing has suggested that gender plays a major role in the ability to correctly process human facial emotion. The purpose of the research presented in this dissertation has three goals: first, an attempt to determine if gender is significant in reaction to facial affect; second, to address the question of whether a distractor plays a role in the processing of facial expression; and third, an attempt to understand the information systems implications involved in such a study.

Multimedia, while still in its infancy, is recognized as the wave of the future. The research conducted in this study furthers the efforts of multimedia in that significant evidence has been found to indicate that males and females respond differently when faced with the same stimuli. Further, evidence shows that the subject may be more positively responsive to like faces (male/male and female/female). This research gives us the ability to fine tune the multimedia instruments of the future to create more favorable conditions in subjects working with computers, etc.

Research indicates that primitive processing of faces is efficient in that it may be automatic and may appear early enough in development to be qualify as being innate. Moreover, a substantial body of research suggests that facial displays of emotion possess the properties requisite for the development of automatic processing, even if it is not innate (Barrera & Maurer, 1981; LaBarbera, Izard, Vietze, & Parisi, 1976; Schwartz, Izard, & Ansul 1985; Wilcox & Clayton, 1968; Ekman, 1982; Izard, 1971). Facial displays of emotion clearly have the necessary properties for the development of automatic processing: Displays are available and consistently associated with specific emotions across individuals and cultures (Hansen & Hansen, 1988).

Extensive study has addressed the parameters of automatic or preattentive processing and it has been described extensively, (e.g., Bargh, 1984; Logan, 1979; Shiffrin & Schneider, 1977; Cheng, 1985; Kahneman & Treisman, 1983; Schneider & Shiffrin, 1985; Treisman, 1982; Treisman & Patterson, 1984; Treisman & Souther, 1985). These properties imply that automatic processing is less (if at all) susceptible to distraction and to information load. Preattentive processing has been defined as a *filtering of information so that some features or aspects of an array are "passed through" and others are "filtered out." By way of this automatic processing, a feature passed through is more likely to come to attention than one filtered out: It would seem to the (attentive) individual as if that feature of the array commanded attention; it would appear to "pop out" from the array (Treisman, 1982; Treisman & Gelade, 1980; Treisman & Paterson, 1984; Treisman & Souther, 1985)* (Hansen & Hansen, 1988). The implication is that the properties of automatic or preattentive processing is said to be more rapid than attentive processing and, unlike attentive processing, may be parallel rather than serial and may not be capacity limited (Hansen and Hansen, 1987).

Ekman (1972) and Friesen (1972) found evidence of the universality of facial expressions. Izard (1971) added evidence that cross-cultural agreement was preserved for most emotions when subjects were allowed to choose their own words to describe feelings shown in facial expressions.

Chapter One

THE FACE

The face is an important avenue of nonverbal expression for several reasons. It is important first because of the amount of information it can convey, especially in a short period of time. Second, it is important because of the kinds of information that can be communicated (emotion, and attitude). Another important factor has been suggested by researchers who believe that there is a broader theoretical import to the relevance of facial behavior. They see facial expressions as an innate characteristic of man, cutting across cultures. Faces serve as signals for underlying emotional states through their portrayal of facial expression. The classification of facial expressions is a necessary prerequisite for the inference of emotion (Bruce, 1988).

Ekman and Friesen (1978) have produced a comprehensive system for describing all possible visually distinguishable movements of the face. The system, called 'The Facial Action Coding System,' or FACS, is based on the enumeration of all the 'action units' of the face which give rise to visible facial movements. An action unit is very roughly equivalent to a particular muscle in the face, whose activations give rise to a noticeable facial change. The correspondence between action units and muscle units is approximate because some muscles give rise to more than one action unit. The basis for these applications are experimental studies that involve emotional determination tasks. Further research (Purcell & Stewart, 1986) described a direct test of the effects of stimulus configuration on perception, the *face-detection effect*, referred to as the FDE. The basis of which posited that the detectability of a stimulus is affected not only by its psychophysical properties (luminance, area, etc.), but also by its informational properties (whether the stimulus forms a pattern that is meaningful for the observer).

Reviewing such studies, Ekman, Friesen, and Ellsworth (1982B) suggest that observers can, at the least, accurately distinguish positive from negative emotional states from facial information.

The idea of innate and universal facial expressions that have links with human emotions was given the scientific hypothesis by Darwin. In Darwin's 1872 work, *THE EXPRESSION OF THE EMOTIONS IN MAN AND ANIMALS,* he offered the notion that emotions were expressed in similar ways among species. He theorized that expressive behaviors have survival value and that they are, therefore, selected much the same as physical structures and characteristics are selected. This idea has been substantiated by the work of ethnologists who have studied man as well as animals (Harper, Wiens, and Matarazzo, 1978).

Darwin chose a comparative approach in his study of emotion, examining the facial expressions of animals, especially primates, to discover the origin of expressive movements in man. This approach fit with his belief in evolution. Darwin concluded that in animals, as in man, facial expressions convey how the animal feels. He considered the expression of emotions essential to the welfare of group-living species, since expressions involve all social interactions and make them possible (Ekman, 1973: 11-12).

FACIAL EXPRESSION

Considerable research has been conducted in recent times on the subject of facial expressions and how they communicate as part of a general interest in nonverbal behavior. Harper, Wiens, and Matarazzo (1978) set forth some of the requirements for such research, stating that research on facial expressions can be organized in the form of various questions. The first deals with what we mean by the term emotion. Much of the early work in this field dealt with attempts to identify and define either distinct categories of emotion or dimensions that were posited to underlie various emotion categories. Another question concerns whether facial components are differentially important in expression of feelings. Most real-life judgments about emotion are made in social settings, so the contribution of contextual clues must be considered carefully.

Contextual clues used by Ekman and O'Sullivan included videotaped, dynamic presentations of faces judged in the context of voice and body. Presentations were made out of that context as well, with observers informed and not informed about the entire social context (Ekman and O'Sullivan, 1988)

Buck et al. (1972) consider the communication of affect through spontaneous facial expression, noting that emotional states are associated with expressive nonverbal facial expressions and gestures. Many researchers have suspected the ability of the individual to express and interpret nonverbal messages and consider this an important factor in his ability to communicate with others. Early studies were unsuccessful because they employed static photographs of posed emotional expressions. Buck (1972) tried to study nonverbal communication in man with an adaptation of the "cooperative conditioning" approach developed to study the nonverbal communication of affect in monkeys. This method involves the presentation of a conditioning stimulus to one of a pair of animals who is the "sender". (The sender responds positively or negatively to a stimulus, thereby conveying or transmitting an emotion to the second animal.) The second animal is the "observer" (The observer is the receptor of the stimuli). In the study, emotional responses were produced through the presentation of emotionally loaded visual stimuli. The researchers found that female pairs were more effective in the transmission and reception of nonverbal emotional cues than were the male pairs. It was uncertain whether this was due to a more overt and "readable" nonverbal signal from the female senders than from the male senders or to a heightened sensitivity to nonverbal cues by the female observers. Indeed, both factors could be involved. Both male and female pairs showed negative relationships between the physiological responding of the sender subject and the accuracy of communication. (Buck, 1972). In other words, the skin conductance responses, pleasantness measures and the sender's heart rate acceleration, among other physical responses, revealed a negative correlation between communication accuracy and physical reactions (Buck, Miller, & Caul, 1974). Or, the emotional cues of the subject's face and the biofeedback information do not accurately show a correlation between the expression exhibited and the subject's physical reactions to the display.

The meaning of cues given by facial expressions has been in some dispute among researchers, and they often try to determine how observers make distinctions and determine the meaning of a given cue. Ekman and Friesen (1974) consider the detection of deception from the body or face. They set forth two hypotheses concerning differences between the face and body when a person is engaged in deception. The first hypothesis was confirmed— the face was mentioned more often than the body when subjects were asked what behavior should be censored or controlled in perpetrating deception. The second hypothesis held that when deceptive behavior was judged, more accurate judgments would be made from the body than from the face, but that when honest behavior was judged, there would be little difference in the accuracy achieved from the face or body. This was partially supported by the research (Freisen, 1974).

Watson (1972) considered the influence of contextual cues on the communication of affect through facial expressions, noting: "*Of particular the*

*investigation interest has been of the interaction of facial expression and con-
textual or situational cues on the judgment of affect. Often in an attempt to
determine which set of cues was primarily responsible for providing information about emotion."* Ekman, Friesen and Ellsworth (1971) noted the
methodological problems prevalent in the area of the judgment of emotion from facial and contextual cues, holding that earlier researchers had
drawn unwarranted and unfounded conclusions in that they have failed to
specify the relevant parameters of the phenomena. In other words, other
research failed to take into account image, method of image display, image
context, subject environments, and other potentially pertinent detail. In
response to this fact, Ekman et al. (1971) formulated appropriate methodological guidelines. Any judgment of combinations must include source
clarity or the amount or type of information about emotion available to
observers when they are exposed to a single source, the distinct emotions
associated with each source, and the pairing of sources to yield concordant
and discordant combinations. Ekman's guidelines require that the source
image be distinct, the information to be conveyed must be unmistakable,
and the subject-image combinations must be paired and described when
producing concordant and discordant combinations.

Arnoff, Woike and Hyman (1992) examined the stimulus patterns
formed by angry and happy faces to determine which patterns convey the
meaning of threat or warmth. Usually an angry expression shows two eye-
brows turned down forming a V-shaped geometric pattern, i.e. a reduced
roundness. Their results suggested that a small set of primary geometric
features, which include increased roundness, and decreased linearity, diag-
onality and angularity of the form, is the visual information that bolsters
the meaning of warmth that is perceived in the visual pattern, whereas the
reverse set of geometric information induces a meaning of threat (Arnoff,
Woike and Hyman, 1992.)

DECODING NONVERBAL CUES

In studies by Stanners, Byrd and Gabriel (1985), there was strong evidence to show that females identified pleasant female facial expressions more quickly than any other target/subject combination. Zajonc's studies (1980) argue that a decision is based on an early affective (like-dislike) reaction to the image rather than a feature discrimination process. Hansen and Hansen (1988) studies, using one angry face in a happy crowd or one happy face in an angry crowd, theorized that a preattentive, parallel search for a feature would be relatively insensitive to distraction whereas an attentive search, entailing serial shifts of focus, would be susceptible for distraction (Bargh, 1982, 1984; Bargh & Pietromonaco, 1982; Shiffrin & Schneider, 1977; Treisman, 1982; Treisman & Peterson, 1984; Treisman & Souther, 1985). In fact, their studies showed that the *detection and location of a feature can be accomplished preattentively, whereas discrimination requires attentional processing* (Bergen & Julesz, 1983; Cheesman & Merikle, 1986; Sagi & Julesz, 1985a, 1985b). *An angry face could be detected and located in a happy crowd, but its content—that is was, in fact, an angry face—could not be discriminated preattentively.*

FACE PROCESSING

Face processing engages several separately localized cognitive mechanisms. According to Hillger and Koenig (1991), there is evidence that separate left- and right-hemisphere mechanisms are involved in face processing. Some of them appear to be general-purpose visual mechanisms that are more efficient in the left-hemisphere, whereas others appear to be specialized (though not necessarily face-specific) mechanisms that are more efficient in the right hemisphere. The left-hemisphere seemed able to detect differences in single facial features (parsing). These mechanisms are probably engaged simultaneously when a stimulus is presented; the mechanism that is most appropriate for the judgment wins—i.e. produces a response faster and more accurately (Hillger and Koenig, 1991).

Information about the features present in a face are important for its perception and recognition. Evidence was found in an experiment by Bruce, Doyle, Dench, and Burton (1991), for featural information in face recognition. Subjects were shown computer-generated images of faces and houses with the same features but different spatial configurations. The subjects abstracted the prototype for each set. This tendency to identify the prototype as the most familiar was greater for faces than for houses. Implications are that faces may be processed differently than other familiar images.

The components of facial communication (nonverbal expressions, physiological reactivity, and self-reports) were considered by Zuckerman et al (1981). They note that two different models have been advanced concerning the role of facial expression in the experience of emotion. The first is the facial feedback hypothesis that states that facial expressions regulate affective experience, a position that has been supported by findings that experimentally induced changes in facial expressiveness produced corresponding changes in autonomic responses and self-reports of emotion. In other words, when shown images of negative facial expressions, subjects responded by themselves producing negative facial and emotional feedback (facial expressions as well as emotion).

In Zuckerman's study (1981), the facial feedback hypothesis and the externalizer-internalizer distinction were evaluated through the manipulation of facial expressiveness and the measurement of subsequent autonomic responses and self-reports of emotion. The authors concluded that higher levels of facial expressiveness of the subjects were accompanied by higher levels of autonomic activity and subjective reports of affective experience.

Conversely, the second model posits that expressive behavior and responses are negatively related, (the biofeedback responses indicate little physical response for facially expressive people while less facially responsive subjects exhibited more physical reactions) and there is evidence supporting this view in correlational analysis showing that facially expressive people (externalizers) exhibit less autonomic arousal than do those who are not facially expressive (internalizers). That is, facially expressive people are less likely to respond physically than non-facially expressive people. There are three commonly assessed components of emotional states which are considered here—nonverbal expressions, physiological reactivity, and self-reports.

Some researchers have examined the relationship between facial expression and other physiological changes caused by emotional response. Notarius et al.(1982) state that the relationship among facial displays of emotion, subjective experience of affect, and physiological response to emotional stimuli is central to all theories of emotion. They feel that several factors appear to affect the relationship among facial expression, physiological reactivity, and self-report of emotion and to underlie discrepant findings across studies. In their own study, they explore the relationships among facial displays of emotion, subjective experience of affect, and physiological reactivity in a situation meeting certain criteria. Faced with a potent interpersonal stressor, extreme anger or rage, for examples minimal facially expressive subjects displayed a significant heart rate increase, appraised the stressor situation as more threatening, and self-reported feeling more guilt than did subjects who were very expressive.

GENDER DIFFERENCES

Studies by Rotter and Rotter (1988) indicate that the female has a superior ability to recognize facial expressions of emotion. These studies were conducted using photographs of male and female faces displaying anger, fear, sadness and disgust. These studies seem to further indicate that females are more accurate at revealing emotion than the male. The single exception being anger, which was more readily recognized when expressed by men than by women. Additionally, it has been found that females identify facial expression more accurately than males (Hall, 1978). It might also be expected that females are able to identify expressions more rapidly than males (Stanners, Byrd, Gabriel, 1985). The implication of the Stanners, Byrd and Gabriel study being that females (relative to males) have some specialized capacity for processing female faces.

Davitz (1964) and Tagiuri (1969) hypothesized that the "gender effect" (a term they coined to explain the gender encoding/decoding capabilities of the male versus female) varied appreciably with the gender of the sender (or target, as referenced in this study). However, in Hall's later study (1978), it was found that the gender effect did not vary with the gender of the sender (or target). According to Hall, "*the direction of the effect is consistent with gender role stereotypes* (e.g. Broverman, Vogel, Broverman, Clarkson, & Rosenkrantz, 1972*), and it is possible that females learn early....*"how a girl ought to act." *This learning would probably not directly produce a performance advantage in judging nonverbal cues, but over time the added motivation to relate to others expressively and practice at attending to interpersonal expression might result in females' superior judging ability.*"

Hall further postulated that, "*Another kind of explanation, in its simplest form, would hold that females are "wired" from birth to be especially sensitive to nonverbal cues. This would make evolutionary sense, because nonverbal sensitivity on a mother's part might enable her to detect distress in her youngsters or threatening signals from other adults, thus enhancing the survival chances of her offspring.*"

In Hall's (1984) review, she notes that females exceed males at all ages in their recognition of emotions and that women are also better senders (facial transmitters) of emotion than men (Buck, Miller, Caul, 1974; Buck, 1979; Hall, 1984; Kirouac and Dorè, 1985).

Kirouac and Dorè (1984) tested the judgment of facial expression of six emotions (happiness, surprise, fear, sadness, disgust, and anger) as a function of gender and level of education. Their results showed that overall, the recognition of emotions was very good. However, there were strong differences between emotions and gender and this confirmed previous reports that women are better than men in decoding facial expressions of emotion.

Buck and Miller (1974) explored possible relationships between gender and personality variables and the negative correlation between communication accuracy and physiological responding, as previously explained. The study demonstrated significant communication of emotion via facial expression using both the categorization and pleasantness measures of communication accuracy. The results indicated that the superior communication found among female pairs was due to the greater facial responsiveness of the female senders. Female senders demonstrated more accurate communication than male senders, but female observers were not found to be reliably more accurate than male observers. Females were also rated as being more facially expressive than males. Males had a tendency to be internalizers while females tended to be externalizers. This was related to cultural influences, since in our society males are generally discouraged from overly expressing most emotions than are girls.

Research pertaining to gender differences in judgment accuracy for negative facial expressions presents contradictory results. For example, Rosenthal, Hall, DiMatteo, Rogers and Archer (1979), using the Profile of Nonverbal Sensitivity (PONS), reported a significant three-way interaction among decoder (receiver of stimuli) gender, dominance, and positivity of cues. In decoding negative facial images, females are better at recognizing negative cues than males, but their advantage is weaker for negative dominant cues (i.e., jealous rage) than for negative submissive cues (asking for forgiveness). Research has shown that men generally tend to externalize feelings of aggression or anger while women tend to internalize those emotions. Gitter, Black, and Mostofsky (1972) found no evidence of gender differences in males' and females' ability to decode various expressions. Haviland and Ingate (1980), however, reported some preliminary findings which suggest that males were perceptually vigilant for expressions of distress (negative submissive cues) (Rotter 1988).

The idea that women respond to emotional stimuli by an activation of emotion processing systems, and men respond with a reactive inhibition is suggested in the research by Burton and Levy (1989). Their data showed that reaction times to negative emotions are faster overall than to positive emotions. A number of studies that suggest that women are more emotionally expressive than men (Buck et all, 1972, 1974, 1982; Kemper, 1978a, 1978b; Lewis, 1976, 1983; Miller, 1976; Mitchel, 1974; Strouse, 1974). Burton and Levy found that response times to negative emotions take longer in the right visual field than in the left visual field, whereas response times to positive emotions are longer in the left visual field. The effect was found to be significant among females but not among males. They suggested that the intensity of induced emotion may be greater for females than males due to the elaborative responses in females and the reactive, inhibitory responses in men.

In a face-to-face task, comparisons of a centrally presented and a laterally presented emotional face were required. The Emotional Valence (positive or negative response) by Visual Field Interaction (left visual field or right visual field) testing found that reaction times in the left visual field were faster for negative emotions presented in the left visual field. In addition, reaction times to positive emotions were faster when presented in the right visual field. An interaction of gender, task, and emotional valence was found. There were opposite effects for the two genders (Burton & Levy). The reasons for the opposite responses is that there is generally a greater right hemisphere superiority for women for expressing facial emotion. The right cerebral hemisphere is specialized for interpretation and communication of emotion (Landis, Assol, and Perret, 1979; Safer and Levanthal, 1977; Strauss and Moscovitch, 1981). If this is true, then it follows that females should respond more quickly and accurately than males in an emotion identification task.

The existence of sex differences in hemispheric laterality remains a controversial subject. Women often outperform men on tasks of spatial abilities (Benbow & Stanley, 1980; McGone, 1980; Springer & Deutsch, 1989).

Among right-handed subjects, men have generally shown more extensive later-alization of language within the left hemisphere and spatial functions within the right hemisphere. Women have typically been described has having a more diffuse and bilateral representation of language and spatial faculties when compared with men (Bradshaw & Nettleton, 1983; McGone, 1980; Springer & Deutsch, 1989) (Harrison, Gorelczenko & Cook, 1990).

In the Harrison et al studies evidence was found that indicated that left visual field presentations resulted in superior overall response times, irrespective of the affective valence of the stimulus of the gender of the subject. They also found evidence of overall better recognition for the positive emotions as compared to the negative emotions across visual half-fields. Additionally, men showed superior emotional identification with the left visual field while women did not. Their study indicated that men were faster than women in attempts to *tap right hemisphere identification of facial expressions. On the surface, then, it would appear that the results support the contention of a more diffuse lateralization among women for the processing of affective information.* (Harrison et al, 1990).

In a study by Erwin et al, evidence was found that male subjects, as compared to female subjects, were selectively less sensitive to sad emotion in female faces. Female subjects were more sensitive overall to emotional expression in male faces than in female faces. In their study men and women differed in performance depending on the gender of the facial stimuli (Erwin, Gur, Gur, Skolnick, Mawhinney-Hee, & Smailis, 1992).

Further, they found that women are generally more sensitive to happy than sad faces and are more sensitive to male than female faces, whereas men are equally sensitive to happy and sad faces in men but substantially less sensitive to sadness in women's faces. Analysis of their results lead them to conclude that controlling for the gender of the facial image displayed moderated the male advantage. They suggested further study in the relationship of gender between the displayed image and the subject.

This research poses the question of whether the subjects' gender effect is independent of the gender of the stimulus face. In other words, does the gender of the displayed image play a role in the response of the subject? Hugdahl, Inverson and Johnson, (1993) discovered that male faces were overall better recognized than female faces, and particularly the negative male face. Male negative faces also required longer VRTS (visual response time—the time required from the initial display of the facial information to the identification of the facial expression as negative or positive). For the VRT data, the female positive stimulus face was identified more rapidly than other stimulus faces.

DISTRACTORS

To achieve a communication function, facial movements have to be rapidly processed and decoded. (Kirouac and Dorè, 1984) In their study Kirourac and Dorè used slides prepared in Ekman's *Pictures of Facial Affect* to test the responses of 20 university students. They used six emotions (happiness, surprise, disgust, anger, sadness and fear) and required each of the subjects to press one of six keys corresponding to the emotion displayed on the screen. Their results showed that humans can accurately abstract emotional information from facial stimuli available for extremely short intervals. Included in their procedures were visual masks (visual masking is a technique used in detection experiments that theoretically interferes with the processing of an image or the reduction of the visibility of one stimulus, called the target, by a spatio-temporally overlapping or adjacent second stimulus, called the mask) which quickly followed the target face (Tassone, 1992). In other work by Purcell and Stewart (1986), targets consisted of conventional faces and distorted faces, each of which was followed by a patterned masking distractor.

In Russell and Fehr's (1987) work, the context idea was taken slightly further and they designed an experiment to study the relational character of judgment, as described by different theories of how the stimulus context provides a frame of reference anchoring the scale of judgment. Context includes the medium upon or through which the image is displayed, any background surrounding the image, auditory clues accompanying the image, or any other added dimension which further adds to or detracts from the displayed image itself. *"The judgment of a facial expression is not fixed by its particular physical features but rather depends on how it compares with other expressions. The relational character of affective judgments has been demonstrated in studies of various stimuli, including studies of the judged intensity of happy and sad faces."*

In studies by Hansen and Hansen (1988) experiments were designed that furthered the research on distractor and context work. Their experiments consisted of displays containing all happy faces, all angry faces, an angry face in a crowd of happy faces, and a happy face in an angry crowd. Their initial experiment neither proved nor disproved their theory, but pointed to an explanation that variations in the faces disguised the presence of a face showing a discrepant (differing) emotion. They, therefore, amended their experiment to use photographs of the same individual with either a happy or an angry face. Results from the second experiment showed that subjects took less time to locate the angry face in the happy crowd than the happy face in the angry crowd. Their experiments were designed to test the hypothesis that face-processing is oriented toward threat detection and that facial expression processing is a preattentive process in some cases. Their results indicated that the angry faces were found in larger crowds in approximately the same time intervals as in the smaller crowds. They further found that *"detection and location of a feature can be accomplished preattentively, whereas discrimination requires attentional processing. An angry face could be detected and located in a happy crowd, but its content—that it was, in fact, an angry face—could not be discriminated preattentively"* (Hansen & Hansen (1988).

INTERFACE ISSUES

Judgment

Judgment is generally defined as the process of forming an opinion or reaching a conclusion on the available material. The mental act of comparing or evaluating choices within a given set of values, frequently with the purpose of choosing a course of action. Research in nonverbal communication tasks very often requires the use of observers, coders, raters, decoders, or judges. (Dictionary of Behavioral Science, 1973.)

Affect

Affect is a general term used more or less interchangeably with various others such as emotion, feeling, mood. Historically the term has various more specialized usages. At one point it was considered to be one of the three 'mental functions' along with cognition and volition. Later it was used as a label for the pleasantness/unpleasantness dimension of feeling. (Dictionary of Behavioral Science, 1973.)

More specifically, affects are sets of muscular and glandular responses located in the face which generate sensory feedback that is either acceptable or unacceptable, that is, the feedback generates a positive or negative response in the viewer. The affect system provides the primary blueprints for cognition, decision and action. The affect system is, therefore, the primary innate biological motivating mechanism (Ekman, 1978a).

An understanding of the breakdown of the concepts of cognition and perception are required in order to fully understand the interface issues encountered by the human factors specialists.

User interface is a term from computer science, referring to the hardware, the command language syntax and the dialogue of interaction with the user. *User interface* is viewed as an important and integral part of the total design and influences the design of other system components. The term *human factors* (user interface, man-machine communications are aspects of human factors) describes a field of research, concerned with all aspects of the use of machinery by humans and the implications for the design of that machinery. Most of the research in **human factors** has to do with quantifiable data on such topics as stress, noise levels in the work place and visual activity.

Human factors specialists must incorporate both the technical and human aspects in their designs, allowing greater flexibility in what, why and how people work. The technological design changes the way in which the workers communicate with the system and their ideas to one another. Information systems increasingly alter relationships, patterns of communication and perceived influence and control (Keen, 1986).

Ergonomics is closely associated with the term human factors. **Ergonomics** is concerned with designing for human use. This is also referred to as **human engineering**. The design of the equipment to meet the needs of human capabilities. Topics, such as, the tilt of a display screen, or the design of a chair for a terminal operator, would be ergonomic considerations.

Man-machine communication also derives its origin from computer science, and reflects the advances made in hardware to facilitate interaction with computer users: various pointing devices, a wide range of display technologies, speech input and output.

Human-computer interaction, therefore, is used to refer to all the factors which influence and affect design of interactive systems.

The major human factors problems associated with designing human-computer interactive systems are within the areas of perceptual and cognitive psychology. Their central concern is the process by which we recognize varied instances of a familiar class of objects.

Chapter Two

EXPERIMENT Ia: 50 SUBJECT STUDY
25 FEMALES / 25 MALES
METHOD

A small pilot study began to show the emergence of significance towards gender affect in computer displays. However, in order to justify any significance, it was necessary to increase the population size for a more accurate assessment.

Similar experiments were conducted by Dr. Dean Purcell in the Psychology Department at the University of Oakland, Michigan. The major problem he encountered was a lack of male volunteers.

Independent variables in the experiments conducted in this study included target affect (TA), distractor affect (DA), target gender (TG). The dependant variable was the reaction time.

Fifty undergraduates at an inner city college in Jersey City, New Jersey, participated. Twenty-five of the subjects were male and the other twenty-five subjects were female. No data were collected on race, ethnicity, or religion. The median age was 21. The subjects were a selection made possible through an advertisement in the college newspaper.

METHOD:

In this experiment, two faces were presented simultaneously, one the target face, one the distractor face. The subject was instructed to concentrate on the center face identifying the emotion displayed on the screen.

In the task of studying emotional cues, each subject named the affect of the center face of the two faces presented. These faces are digitized replications of Ekman's faces. The graphic quality of the faces used in this study are similar to the pictures found in a newspaper.

The subjects were instructed to respond by depressing the numeric 4 on the keyboard for an angry face and the numeric 6 for a happy face. After the subject's response, there was a wait period, which required the subject to respond by clicking the return key in order to begin the next test sequence.

The experimenter presented pictures of faces to the subjects on a monitor. The experiment was controlled by a computer running the program *Vscope* in the faculty Computer Science Center. *Vscope* is a software product developed by James T. Enns and Ronald A. Resnick at the Department of Psychology at the University of British Columbia, Vancouver, BC, Canada.

PROCEDURE:

The experimenter told the subjects that they would be participating in an experiment to determine the emotional content from a series of computer imaged faces. On each trial, two faces would appear on the screen simultaneously for a duration period of five (5) milliseconds. One face would appear in the center of the screen and the other face to the left or right of the center. The task of the subjects was to evaluate the emotion expressed by the face in the center portion of the screen as quickly as possible. The faces were pictures of a person smiling or frowning and were either happy or angry. The subjects would register their responses by depressing the number four (4) key on the numeric keypad for angry and the number six (6) key for happy. After the response had been registered on the computer, the screen would clear with a message indicating to the subjects to press any key to continue the process. The subjects' tryout sessions served as a warm-up and were not part of the design. The software internally recorded whether the subject named the correct emotional trait and the associated response time.

The experiments were conducted in the faculty workroom at an inner city college. This provides a well-lighted, quiet, private environment for the subject. The subjects were all seated a uniform distance (60 centimeters) from the computer screen. Random selections of the faces, made by the computer selection process, were presented to the subjects. The selections were broken down into eight blocked segments. They were instructed that the entire experiment would take approximately twenty minutes.

The subjects were administered a consent form and the following instructions:

In these experiments you will have to make decisions concerning the faces, which you will see on the screen. The presentation will be brief approximately five (5) milliseconds. Two faces will appear simultaneously on the screen. The presentation will be preceded by a small cross-hairs indicating the center of the screen. You will focus on the center face. You will then choose whether the face is happy or angry. After the presentation of the face, please make your selection by pressing the #4 key on the number pad for angry and the #6 key for happy. Please respond as quickly and accurately as possible. To familiarize yourself with this procedure, the first series of facial displays are practice trials and not part of the actual study. At the end of the practice, I will stop you and set you up for the actual study. Any questions?

RESULTS AND DISCUSSION:

The data were compiled and descriptive statistics were generated to test the subject's response time, target affect, distractor affect, and gender of target. Repeated-measures of analysis of variance suggested a statistical difference in judgment associated with the independent variables.

General results for female subjects, with variables, Dsr*Gnr, yielded $F(1,23)= 4.704$, p < .05, and with variables Trt*Gnr, yielded $F(1,23)=4.043$,p < .06. General results for male subjects, with variables, Trt*Dsr*Gnr, yielded $F(1,25)= 0.369$, p<.06, began to indicate a pattern wherein the distractor appeared to play a role in the test results. Both genders showed a quicker response time when processing a happy face of the same gender. Male response times were faster, overall, than female response times.

Both male and female results showed the fastest times when the target face and the distractor face were both happy. It was not until analysis of the data was being done that the researcher discovered that no measures had been taken for the gender of the subject on an individualized basis. Thus, the reaction times recorded, while measured on an overall average for males and females as separate groups, had not been recorded for the gender of the subject. In addition, the researcher was not convinced that the population size of the study was large enough to adequately allow interpretation on a generalized basis.

The experiment, therefore, was amended to include the gender of each subject as well as the gender of the target and distractor faces as well as to increase the population size. To increase the population size, an additional 50 subjects were chosen who had not taken part in the previous experiment. By disallowing repeat testing, the researcher wanted to avoid an unwanted familiarity with the same facial images. In addition, a third area of study was also included, the percentage of correct responses, allowing a more in-depth understanding of the subjects' recorded responses.

RESULTS FOR FACTOR
Target Affect*Distractor Affect*Target Gender
FEMALE SUBJECTS ONLY
Coefficients
Expected Cell Means of : Means<Response Time> on Trt*Dst*Gnr

Level Of Trt*Dsr*Gnr	Expected Cell Mean	Cell Count
T.Angry,D.Angry,Female	737.7	24
T.Happy,D.Angry,Female	706.9	24
T.Angry,D.Happy,Female	730.5	24
T.Happy,D.Happy,Female	**703.5**	**24**
T.Angry,D.Angry,Male	717.2	24
T.Happy,D.Angry,Male	717.2	24
T.Angry,D.Happy,Male	736.5	24
T.Happy,D.Happy,Male	727.4	24

Note: Response times are in milliseconds.

RESULTS FOR FACTOR
Target Affect*Distractor Affect*Target Gender
MALE SUBJECTS ONLY
Expected Cell Means of : Means<Response Time> on
Trt*Dsr*Gnr

Level Of Trt*Dsr*Gnr	Expected Cell Mean	Cell Count
T.Angry,D.Angry,Female	693.8	26
T.Happy,D.Angry,Female	690.0	26
T.Angry,D.Happy,Female	695.2	26
T.Happy,D.Happy,Female	**678.0**	**26**
T.Angry,D.Angry,Male	704.1	26
T.Happy,D.Angry,Male	**678.5**	**26**
T.Angry,D.Happy,Male	712.3	26
T.Happy,D.Happy,Male	682.2	26

Chapter Three

EXPERIMENT Ib : 100 SUBJECT STUDY
50 FEMALES / 50 MALES
METHOD

This experiment mirrors the first which was specifically designed to determine the role gender plays in the judgment of the affect of computer displayed faces. The greatest significance of Experiment Ib is to ensure the validity of the data by increasing the population. The same stimuli used in Experiment Ia was also used in the second experiment. In the task of judging affect, each subject named the emotional trait of the center face of the two faces presented.

The experimenter presented stimuli to the subjects on a computer running the program, Vscope, in the faculty Computer Science Center. *Vscope* is a software product developed by James T. Enns and Ronald A. Resnick at the Department of Psychology at the University of British Columbia, Vancouver, BC, Canada.

The experimenter told the subjects that they would be participating in an experiment to determine the emotional content from a series of computer imaged faces. On each trial, two faces would appear on the screen for a duration period of five milliseconds. One face would appear in the center of the screen and the other face to the left or right of the center. The task of the subjects was to evaluate the emotional trait of the face in the center portion of the screen as quickly as possible. The emotional traits presented were either happy or angry. The subjects would register their responses by depressing the number four key on the numeric keypad for angry and the number six key for happy. After the response had been registered on the computer, the screen would clear with a message indicating to the subjects to press any key to continue the process. The subjects completed one practice trial, the first of a series of four. The practice or tryout sessions served as a warm-up and were not part of the design. The software internally recorded whether the subject named the correct emotional trait and the associated response time.

A consent form was signed by all subjects as in the initial experiment.

RESULTS AND DISCUSSION:

The repeated-measures of analysis of this experiment are summarized in the following pages. While the findings are somewhat consistent with the first experiment, an increase in population size would allow for more accurate analysis of the data before generalizations could be formulated. The second experiment of fifty would also include an additional independent variable, the subject gender (SG), as well as, target affect (TA), distractor affect (DA), and target gender (TG).

Significant statistical differences in judgment of affect are associated with the independent variables. General results for analysis of variance for mean proportion correct, with variables SG*TA*TG yielded $F(1,98)= 5.869$, $p < .025$ and with variables SG*DA yielded $F(1,98)= 4.043$, $p < .05$. The general results for analysis of variance for median reaction time for variables TA, yielded $F(1,98)= 13.479$, $p < .0005$ and variables

SG*TA*DA, yielded F(1,98)= 4.5109, p<.05 and variables SG*TA*TG, yeilded F(1,98)= 22.664, p< .0001. The general results for analysis of variance for male subjects only with variables Trt, yielded F(1,49)= 7.628, p<.01 and variables Trt*Tgr, yielded F(1,49)=7.809, p <.01. The general results for analysis of variance for female subjects only with variables TrT, yielded F(1,49)= 7.815, p< .01 and variables Trt*Tgr, yielded F(1,49)=11.572, p< .01. Female reaction time was always faster than male reaction time, indicating the preattentive processing affect found in previous studies. The female reaction time for processing of happy female faces with a happy distractor was 7.4 milliseconds faster than with an angry distractor, indicating a slight distraction. The male reaction time was faster for the target displaying a male happy face. Males showed a 5.2 millisecond faster response time when the distractor was angry as compared to happy. The male subjects always responded more quickly to male faces, while females always responded more quickly to female faces.

When comparing correct responses, the females produced the highest proportion correct, regardless of the expression of target or distractor, again pointing toward a preattentive processing affect. The proportions correct for all females were higher than the proportion correct for all male subjects. Both male and female subjects showed a higher percentage correct processing an angry male face. Females also showed a higher percent correct with a happy distractor, while males produced more correct responses when the distractor was angry.

Results of this study led the researcher to alter the subsequent experiment by eliminating the distractor. The reasoning for this being: 1) to prove the distractor did or did not have an affect on response time, 2) to determine whether males, females, neither or both *were* distracted, 3) further investigate the *subject gender/target gender affect*.

Results for factor
Subject Gender* Target Affect *Distractor Affect*Target Gender
Coefficients
Expected Cell Means of Mean Proportion Correct on SG*TA*DA*TG

Level of SG*TA*DA*TG	Expected Cell Mean	Cell Count
S female, T angry, D angry, female	0.9687	50
S male, T angry, D angry, female	0.9707	50
S female, T happy, D angry, female	**0.9671**	**50**
S male, T happy, D angry, female	0.9636	50
S female, T angry, D happy, female	0.9768	50
S male, T angry, D happy, female	0.9631	50
S female, T happy, D happy, female	0.9753	50
S male, T happy, D happy, female	0.9568	50
S female, T angry, D angry, male	0.9770	50
S male, T angry, D angry, male	0.9623	50
S female, T happy, D angry, male	0.9667	50
S male, T happy, D angry, male	0.9714	50
S female, T angry, D happy, male	0.9769	50
S male, T angry, D happy, male	**0.9560**	**50**
S female, T happy, D happy, male	0.9687	50
S male, T happy, D happy, male	0.9700	50

Results for factor Subject Gender*Distractor
Coefficients
Expected Cell Means
Expected Cell Means of Mean Proportion Correct on SG *DA

Level of SG *DA	Expected Cell Mean	Cell Count
S female, D angry	0.9699	200
S male, D angry	0.9670	200
S female, D happy	0.9744	200
S male, D happy	0.9615	200

Interaction plot of Subject gender by Distractor affect.

Cell means

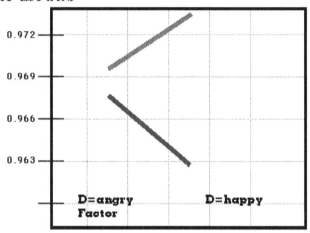

Upper curve female S's
lower curve male S's

Results for Factor
Subject Gender*Distractor Affect*Target Gender
Coefficients
Expected Cell Means of: Mean Proportion Correct on SG*DA*TG

Level of SG*DA*TG	Expected Cell Mean	Cell Count
S female, D angry, female	**0.9679**	**100**
S male, D happy, female	0.9672	100
S female, D happy, female	0.9761	100
S male, D happy, female	0.9600	100
S female, D angry, male	0.9719	100
S male, D angry, male	0.9668	100
S female, D happy, male	0.9728	100
S male, D happy, male	**0.9630**	**100**

Results for factor
Subject Gender*Target Affect*Distractor Affect*Target Gender
Coefficients
Expected Cell Means of: Median<Response Time> on SG*TA*DA*TG

Level of SG*TA*DA*TG	Expected Cell Mean	Cell Count
S female, T angry, D angry, female	685.2	50
S male, T angry, D angry, female	675.1	50
S female, T happy, D angry, female	**649.6**	**50**
S male, T happy, D angry, female	674.4	50
S female, T angry, D happy, female	688.3	50
S male, T angry, D happy, female	676.4	50
S female, T happy, D happy, female	657.1	50
S male, T happy, D happy, female	657.3	50
S female, T angry, D angry, male	670.4	50
S male, T angry, D angry, male	681.4	50
S female, T happy, D angry, male	663.6	50
S male, T happy, D angry, male	**652.1**	**50**
S female, T angry, D happy, male	671.6	50
S male, T angry, D happy, male	691.2	50
S female, T happy, D happy, male	671.5	50
S male, T happy, D happy, male	665.5	50

Interaction of Target affect with Distractor affect.

Anova Male Subjects

Cell means

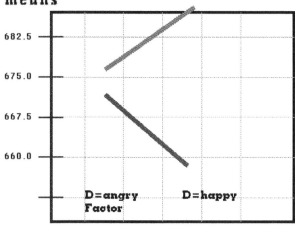

top line is angry target
bottom line is happy target

Cell means

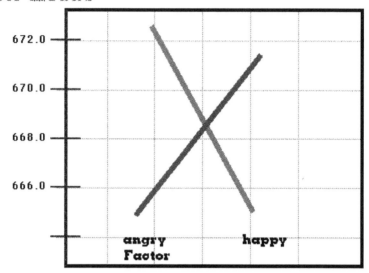

Target Affect X Distractor Affect. x = male °=female

Results for factor Target Affect*Target Gender*Distractor Coefficients
Expected Cell Means of: Median<Response Time> on TA*TG*DA
FEMALES

TA*TG*DA	Expected Cell Mean	Cell Count
angry, female, angry	674.6	50
happy, female, angry	671.8	50
angry, male, angry	680.1	50
happy, male, angry	651.6	50
angry, female, happy	676.0	50
happy, female, happy	656.3	50
angry, male, happy	688.0	50
happy, male, happy	654.0	50

Note: Response times are in milliseconds.

Interaction of Target affect with Distractor affect.

Female subjects only below

Cell means

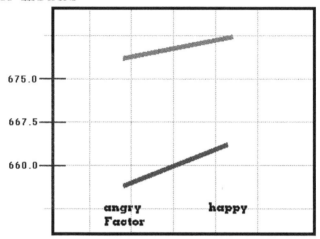

Top line = Angry targets, Bottom line = happy targets.
X axis = Distractor affect.

Target Affect X Target Gender

Cell means

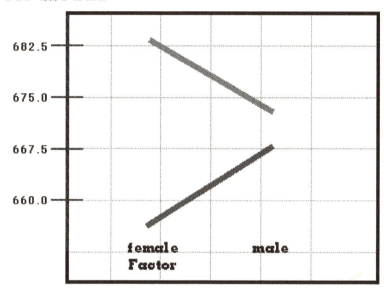

Upper line = angry target.

Lower line = happy target.

X axis = Target Gender.

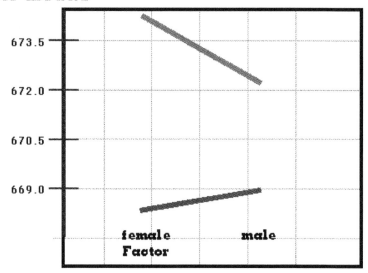

Target Gender by Distracor affect.

Cell means

Upper line = happer distractor.

Results for factor Target Affect*Distractor Affect*Target Gender
Coefficients
Expected Cell Means of: Median<Response Time> on TA*DA*TG
MALES

Level of TA*DA*TG	Expected Cell	Cell Count
angry, angry, female	685.6	50
happy, angry, female	**649.4**	**50**
angry, happy, female	690.2	50
happy, happy, female	658.8	50
angry, angry, male	673.0	50
happy, angry, male	663.2	50
angry, happy, male	672.2	50
happy, happy, male	671.5	50

Note: Response times are in milliseconds.

RESULTS FOR FACTOR
Subject Gender*Target Affect*Distractor Affect*Target Gender
Coefficients
Expected Cell Means of : Means<Response Time> on SG*TA*DA*TG

Level Of SG*TA*DA*TG	Expected Cell Mean	Cell Count
S female, angry, angry, female	727.6	1224
S male, angry, angry, female	731.2	1200
S female, happy, angry, female	698.0	1224
S male, happy, angry, female	714.4	1200
S female, angry, happy, female	734.1	1224
S male, angry, happy, female	723.3	1200
S female, happy, happy, female	**690.6**	**1224**
S male, happy, happy, female	708.2	1200
S female, angry, angry male	713.8	1224
S male, angry, angry, male	742.2	1200
S female, happy, angry, male	706.2	1224
S male, happy, angry, male	**698.2**	**1200**
S female, angry, happy, male	717.4	1224
S male, happy, happy, male	703.4	1224
S male, happy, happy, male	708.6	1200

Note: Response times are in milliseconds.

Chapter Four

EXPERIMENT II: 70 SUBJECT STUDY

This experiment was specifically designed to determine whether the distractor plays a role in the judgment of the affect of computer displayed faces. .The significance of Experiment II is to determine if the subjects are able to respond more quickly to the stimulus face, or if their response times remain approximately the same. Additionally, the amendment of the design of the test was intended to determine whether the subjects were, indeed, distracted by the distractor face.

Seventy additional undergraduates at an inner city college in Jersey City, New Jersey, participated. Thirty-five of the subjects were male and the other thirty-five subjects were female. The subjects participated by random selection. None of the subjects had participated in the initial experiment.

The same stimuli used in Experiments Ia and Ib was used in the second experiment, excepting that the distractor face was removed and only the target face appeared on the computer screen. In the task of judging affect, each subject named the emotional trait of the only face presented.

The experimenter presented stimuli to the subjects on a Macintosh IIsi Apple desk top computer running the program, Vscope, in the faculty Computer Science Center.

On each trial, one face would appear on the screen for a duration period of five milliseconds. The face would appear in the center of the screen. The task of the subjects was to evaluate the emotional trait of the face as quickly as possible. The emotional traits presented were either happy or angry. The subjects would register their responses by depressing the number four (4) key on the numeric keypad for angry and the number six (6) key for happy. After the response had been registered on the computer, the screen would clear with a message indicating to the subjects to press any key to continue the process. The subjects completed one practice trial, the first of a series of four. The practice or tryout sessions served as a warm-up and were not part of the design. The software internally recorded whether the subject named the correct emotional trait and the associated response time.

A consent form was signed by all subjects as in the initial experiment.

RESULTS AND DISCUSSION:

The repeated-measures of analysis of variance of this experiment are summarized in the following tables. Results of the second experiment indicate that the distractor did, indeed, create a distraction for the subjects.

General results for analysis of variance for percent correct with variables SG*Aft, yielded $F(1,68)= 7.800$, $p < .01$. General results of analysis of variance for median reaction time with variables, Aft yielded, $F(1,68)= 13.10$, $p< .001$ and with variables Tg, yielded $F(1,68)= 8.457$, $p <.005$ and with variables Aft*Tg, yielded $F(1,68)= 3.3805$, $p <.01$. The initial design, therefore, should have been more likely to elicit an attentive search when responding to the target stimulus. Results further show that without the distractor, both male and female subjects processed happy male faces most quickly. Happy female faces were second in processing time. Without the distractor, the percentage correct for the affect of the target gender was higher for an angry male target than the other target affects.

ANOVA results for the affect of the target gender showed a significant difference when comparing male and female subject responses. While the male subject probability measured 0.4355, the female subject probability measured only 0.0549, not even close to the male subject results. What caused this much difference has not been determined by the research results. This is particularly interesting in light of the fact that this difference in variance was not evidenced as greatly in the first 100 subject results when the distractor was present.

Results for factor Target Affect*Target Gender
Coefficients
Expected Cell Means of: Proportion Correct on TA*TG

Level of TA*TG	Expected Cell Mean	Cell Count
angry, female	0.9554	70
happy, female	0.9586	70
angry, male	0.9646	70
happy, male	0.9580	70

Results for factor Subject Gender*Target Affect*Target Gender
Coefficients
Expected Cell Means of: Proportion Correct on
SG*TA*TG

Level of SG*TA*TG	Expected Cell Mean	Cell Count
female S, angry, female	0.9554	35
male S, angry female	0.9554	35
female S, happy, female	0.9673	35
male S, happy, female	0.9500	35
female S, angry, male	**0.9542**	**35**
male S, angry, male	0.9750	35
female S, happy, male	0.9714	35
male S, happy, male	**0.9446**	**35**

Results for factor Subject Gender*Target Affect*Target Gender Coefficients
Expected Cell Means of: Median<Response Time> on SG*TA*TG

SG*TA*TG	Expected Cell Mean	Cell Count
female S, angry, female	718.0	35
male S, angry female	685.7	35
female S, happy, female	694.3	35
male S, happy, female	659.1	35
female S, angry, male	700.6	35
male S, angry, male	672.9	35
female S, happy, male	**692.7**	**35**
male S, happy, male	**654.5**	**35**

Results for factor Target Affect*Target Gender
FEMALE
Expected Cell Means of: Median<Response Time> on TA*TG

TA*TG	Expected Cell Mean	Cell Count
angry, female	718.0	35
happy, female	694.3	35
angry, male	700.6	35
happy, male	692.7	35

Cell means

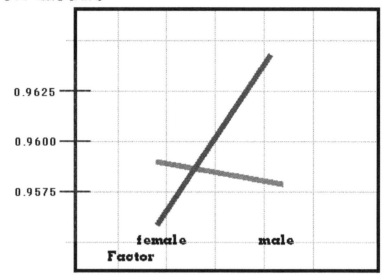

Cell means

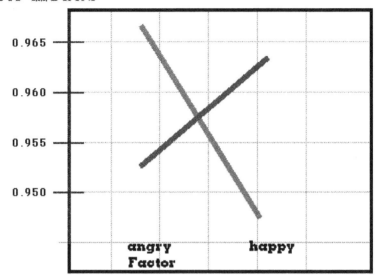

Negative slope = Male subjects
Positive slopes = Female subjects

Results for factor Target Affect*Target Gender
Male
Expected Cell Means of: Median<Response Time> on TA*TG

TA*TG	Expected Cell Mean	Cell Count
angry, female	685.7	35
happy, female	659.1	35
angry, male	672.9	35
happy, male	**654.5**	**35**

Cell means

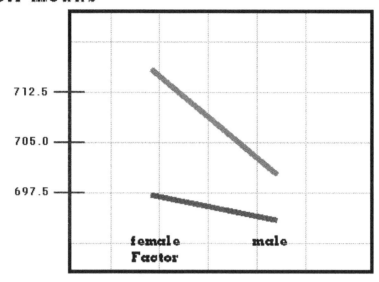

Female Subjects
Top line = angry faces
Bottom line = happy faces

Cell means

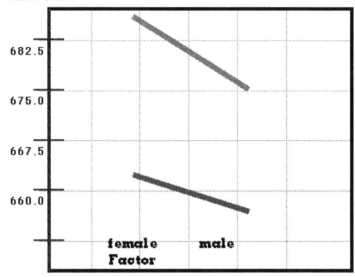

Male Subjects
Top line = Angry Faces
Bottom line = Happy Faces

Chapter Five

GENERAL DISCUSSION

Questions 1 and 2: Is gender significant in reaction to facial affect? and Does a distractor play a role in the processing of facial expression?

Experiments Ia and Ib was designed specifically to determine two things: 1) does the distractor play a role in the response times of the subjects? 2) do humans process faces attentively or preattentively? Experiment Ib was, designed specifically to eliminate the distractor, was intended to determine to what extent the distractor plays a role in processing times and results. The combined results of the experiments were intended to provide an understanding of whether gender is significant in reaction to facial affect, and, if so, to what extent. More importantly, what do the findings mean to the information systems specialist?

Intuitively, it seems that the distractor would, indeed, play a role in distracting the attention of the subject. Results indicate that the distractor does play a role, but not as significantly and not necessarily as originally thought.

Experiment Ia consisted of 50 subjects, 25 male and 25 female. Results of the experiment showed that both male and female subjects processed a happy face most efficiently. Experiment Ib was added to ensure the accuracy of the first results and, as expected, both male and female subjects processed a happy face most efficiently. In both experiments males processed happy male faces more quickly and females processed happy female faces more quickly. Differences in processing times were so minute as to be considered insignificant—there being only a 7.4 millisecond response time difference in favor of the female subjects.

This suggested that angry faces took both male and female subjects longer to process. There is also an indication that the gender of the target played a role in the response times of the subject, each subject gender being led to respond more quickly to the target of the same gender. Results, then, from the combined responses of the first experiment indicate a gender affect for computer displayed faces.

In conducting the second experiment, it was believed that the results would prove to be similar. Somewhat surprisingly, however, results indicated that male subjects were significantly more efficient at processing the displayed faces without the distractor. More unexpectedly, female subjects processed male faces more quickly without the distractor, while their overall average processing time did not change.

From the results of the studies, implications are that females are processing preattentively (in parallel) while males process attentively (in serial). Bargh (1984), Logan (1979), Shiffrin & Schneider (1977), Treisman (1982), among others previously cited, have suggested that the properties of preattentive processing is more rapid than parallel. Studies by Hillger and Koenig (1991) have put forth a plausible explanation as to why this is true. Evidence exists that indicates that separate left and right hemisphere mechanisms are involved in the processing of faces. The left hemisphere is apparently more able to detect differences in single facial features, while the right hemisphere appears to be more specialized in holistic processing and more adapted toward template matching (Hillger & Koenig, 1991).

Because the results of the second experiment did not differ significantly in female response times, (there being a 2.1 millisecond faster response in the first (distractor) experiment when compared to results of the second experiment), the initial implication would appear to be that the female subjects were not distracted by the distractor face.

What becomes more interesting, however, is that in experiment Ia and Ib, male subjects chose happy male faces and female subjects chose happy female faces, while results of the second experiment showed a preference for a happy male face, regardless of subject gender.

In addition, the male subject response time dropped 038.2 milliseconds in the second experiment, the implication being that the male was indeed distracted by the distractor. This would appear to support the argument made by others (Hansen & Hansen, 1988; Bargh & Pietromonaco, 1982; Beck, 1983) that males process attentively (in serial) while females process preattentively (in parallel).

There was no indication that the expression displayed on the face of the distractor played any role in the processing responses of either the male or female subjects. Further evidence was found to support the theory of Ekman, Friesen, and Ellsworth (1982b) that observers can distinguish between positive and negative emotional states, even in the presence of a distractor.

Experiments Ia and Ib would seem to further studies conducted by Stanners, Byrd and Gabriel (1985), that there is strong evidence to show that females identify pleasant female facial expressions more quickly than any other target/subject combination. Experiment II, however, conducted without a distractor, presented an unexpected female preference for happy male faces. This result would point more toward Zajonc's theory of an early affective (like-dislike) reaction to the image, rather than a feature discrimination process.

There remains a question arising from the results of Experiment II as compared to the results of Experiments Ia and Ib. When the target face is the only focal point, meaning that it is within its own context and there is no distractor, why is the male subject response time significantly faster and why does the female subject now choose the happy male face?

Question 3: How can understanding the results of such a study contribute to the information systems implications involved in such a study?

In relating the results of this study to computer information systems, we will first examine cognitive psychology, or how we gain information, how much and how that information is transformed into knowledge and used to direct our attention and behavior. For the male subject, in all experiments, a happy male face was identified more quickly, regardless of distractor. More importantly, when the distractor was eliminated, the male response time dropped significantly. This would imply that a happy male computer image displayed to a male computer user would stimulate production and efficiency in tasks requiring artificial intelligence computer communications with a male subject user. Visual storage of information stemming from an ongoing "conversation" with a male human image on the screen would serve to keep the image on the screen longer, the added stimulus of auditory sensation would further enhance the storage of the information conveyed by the computer.

The perception of a familiar, comfortable face would allow the male user to become accustomed to "conversing" with a familiar face, forcing out the contextual cues and allowing concentration on the target, distinguished from competing normal variation.

From the results of Experiments Ia and Ib, the same would hold true for the female subject faced with a happy female computer displayed image in those instances where there is background information being transmitted (distractors). However, the results of Experiment II indicate that the male user will potentially respond more quickly than a female user, but that both will respond well to a happy male face displayed in a single display environment.

The human factors specialist should bear these findings in mind when engineering and designing not only the user interface to be used by the computer system, but the ergonomics of the system as well.

Research for this dissertation suggests that judgment of the system will be based on the affect it produces in the user, be that male or female. In designing human-computer interactive systems, no longer is a simple Graphical User Interface (GUI) sufficient. The designer should engineer a system that is designed ergonomically to use the graphical human face and expression most likely to cause an efficient, pleasant response in the user.

Given the design specifications (single point of focus versus background distractor information) and the user community (male or female), the computer-displayed face would vary dependent solely on the purpose and user of the specific application.

Conclusions

1. Under the conditions of two computer displayed faces (i.e., target and distractor) presented simultaneously to both male and female subjects, it was found that a happy face was processed more efficiently.
2. Under the same conditions, it was found that males processed happy male faces more quickly and females processed happy female faces more quickly. Each subject, when given a choice, identifies with their own particular gender, indicating a gender affect for computer displayed facial images.
3. Under the conditions of a single computer displayed face presented to both male and female subjects, it was found that the male subjects' average response time decreased significantly without the distractor. Given the same experimental circumstances, however, the female subjects' response time remained approximately the same.

Results indicate that female subjects process facial images in parallel (preattentive processing) while male subjects process facial images serially (attentive processing). Does this evidence point back to Darwin's theory of evolution or the Biblical definition of the male as hunter and female as gatherer and caregiver?

APPLIED RECOMMENDATIONS:

In the design of interactive visual displays, the human factors specialist needs to utilize a happy male face icon in a single display environment for the best overall reaction time, regardless of the gender of the user. Improved response times equate to increased interactivity and productivity for the end-user community.

EXPERIMENTAL RECOMMENDATIONS:

Further study is warranted in several areas, particularly when comparing the ANOVA AFT*TG variances for median response times. In the final experiment, the numbers ranged widely, from 0.4355 for male subject probability time to 0.0549 for subject probability time, with no clear understanding as to why, or what caused the fluctuation.

Additionally, no metrics was taken to measure racial response differences. All faces used in the experiments were Caucasian, while the subjects came from various racial and ethnic backgrounds. It is suggested that response times may improve if the race, as well as gender, of the target match those of the subject.

Other questions raised by this study warrant study as well, for example, would the female subject time remain unchanged with an increase in the number and frequency of distractors? Would male subject response times decline significantly with an increase in the number of distractors?

About the Author

Ralph Reilly holds a Ph.D., from Stevens Institute of Technology in Information Systems, with an emphasis on human computer interaction. His research focused on gender differences in the judgement of affect.

He received his MS from Barry University in Miami, Florida in 1988 and his BS in Computer Science in 1986 also from Barry University. He is an acting Assistant Professor in Management Information Systems, at the University of Hartford. He holds private pilots' license, a second-degree black belt and maintains an active application for the astronaut candidate program at NASA.

Appendices

Appendix A

ANOVA RESULTS
FEMALE SUBJECTS
General Results...........................192 total cases
ANOVA
Analysis of Variance for Means<Response Time>
No Selector

SOURCE PROB	DF	SUM OF SQ	MEAN SQ	F-RATIO	PROB
Const	1	100119150	100119150	1441.6	<=0.0001
Sbj	23	1597370	69450.9		
Trt	1	13451.1	13451.1	2.4288	0.1328
Sbj*Trt	23	127375	5538.06		
Dsr	1	1071.30	1071.30	1.2429	0.2764
Sbj*Dsr	23	19823.9	861.908		
Trt*Dsr	1	86.9796	86.9796	0.12231	0.7297
Sbj*Trt*Dsr	23	16356.6	711.157		
Gnr	1	1158.39	1158.39	0.76507	0.3908
Sbj*Gnr	23	34824.2	1514.09		
Trt*Gnr	1	7127.71	7127.71	4.0432	0.0562
Sbj*Trt*Gnr	23	40546.5	1762.89		
Dsr*Gnr	1	4855.72	4855.72	4.7046	0.0407
Sbj*Dsr*Gnr	23	23738.9	1032.13		
Trt*Dsr*Gnr	1	501.336	501.336	0.44872	0.5096
Sbj*Trt*Dsr*Gnr	23	25696.7	1117.25		
Error	0	0			
Total	191	1913985			

MALE SUBJECTS
General Results..........................208 total cases
ANOVA
Analysis of Variance for Means<Response Time>
No Selector

SOURCE PROB	DF	SUM OF SQ	MEAN SQ	F-RATIO	PROB
Const	1	99531972	99531972	588.45	<=0.0001
Sbj	25	4228542	169142		
Trt	1	19110.7	19110.7	3.7754	0.0634
Sbj*Trt	25	126548	5061.94		
Dsr	1	5.90433	5.90433	0.00587	0.9395
Sbj*Dsr	25	25147.2	1005.89		
Trt*Dsr	1	1047.45	1048.45	1.4263	0.2436
Sbj*Dsr Sbj	25	18359.4	734.375		
Trt*Dsr	1	1047.45	1047.45	1.4263	0.2436
Sbj*Trt*Dsr	25	18359.4	734.375		
Gnr	1	1313.46	1313.46	1.5840	0.2198
Sbj*Gnr	25	20729.8	829.193		
Trt*Gnr	1	3937.65	3937.65	3.1930	0.0861
Sbj*Trt*Gnr	25	30830.2	1233.21		
Dsr*Gnr	1	1649.89	1649.89	1.9843	0.1713
Sbj*Dsr*Gnr	25	20786.8	831.474		
Trt*Dsr*Gnr	1	253.900	253.900	0.36930	0.5489
Sbj*Trt*Gnr	1	19110.7	19110.7	3.7754	0.0634
Dsr*Gnr	25	17188.1	687.523		
Error	0	0			
Total	207	4515450			

General Results
800 total cases
ANOVA
Analysis of Variance For Mean Proportion Correct
No Selector

SOURCE PROB	DF	SUM OF SQ	MEAN SQ	F-RATIO	PROB
Const	1	749.925	749.925	122651	<=0.0001
Sbj	98	0.599203	0.006114		
SG	1	0.012485	0.012485	2.0419	0.1562
TA	98	0.000444	0.000444	0.15493	0.6947
Sbj*TA	1	0.280676	0.002864		
SG*TA	98	0.003048	0.003048	1.0643	0.3048
DA	1	0.000045	0.000045	0.03619	0.8495
Sbj*DA	98	0.122861	0.001254		
SG*DA	1	0.005069	0.005069	4.0436	0.0436
TA*DA	1	0.000197	0.000197	0.16131	0.6888
Sbj*TA*DA	98	0.119891	0.001223		
SG*TA*DA	1	0.000040	0.000040	0.0358	0.8571
TG	1	0.000146	0.000146	0.06698	0.7963
Sbj*TG	98	0.213910	0.002183		
SG*TG	1	0.000049	0.000049	0.02253	0.8810
TA*TG	1	0.001380	0.001380	0.96610	0.3281
Sbj*TA*TG	98	0.139950	0.001428		
SG*TA*TG	1	9,998382	0.008382	5.8699	0.0172
DA*TG	1	0.000192	0.000192	0.25149	0.6172
Sbj*DA*TG	98	0.074692	0.000762		
SG*DA*TG	1	0.001393	0.001393	1.8277	0.1795
TA*DA*TG	1	0.000112	0.000112	0.08129	0.7762
Sbj*TA*DA*TG	98	0.135600	0.001384		
SG*TA*DA*TG	1	0.000017	0.000017	0.01195	0.9132
Error	0	0			
Total	799	1.71978			

General Results
ANOVA
Analysis of Variance for Median <Response Time>
No Selector
800 total cases
Note: Trt= Target Affect, Tgr= Target Gender, Dsr= Distractor Affect

SOURCE	DF	SUM OF SQ	MEAN SQ	F-RATIO	PROB
Const	1	359168242	359168242	3106.9	<=0.0001
Sbj	98	11329224	115604		
SG	1	106.580	106.580	0.00092	0.9758
TA	*1*	*78645.8*	*78645*	*13.479*	*0.0004*
Sbj*TA	98	571781	5834.50		
SG*TA	1	380.880	380.880	0.06528	0.7989
DA	1	907.380	907.380	0.70779	0.4022
Sbj*DA	98	125636	1282.00		
SG*DA	1	1529.05	1529.04	1.1927	0.2775
TA*DA	1	581.405	581.405	0.65337	0.4209
Sbj*TA*DA	98	87205.6	889.853	889.853	
*SG*TA*DA*	*1*	*4014.08*	*4014.08*	*4.5109*	*0.0362*
TG	1	117.811	117.811	0.06897	0.7934
Sbj*TG	98	167408	1708.25		
SG*TG	1	0.001250	0.001250	0.00000	0.9993
TA*DA	1	667.951	667.951	0.43889	0.5092
Sbj*TA*TG	98	1521.90			
*SG*TA*TG*	*1*	*34492.5*	*34492.5*	*22.664*	*<=0.0001*
DA*TG	1	2356.41	2356.41	2.3882	0.1255
Sbj*DA*TG	98	966693.6	986.669		
SG*DA*TG	1	2914.66	2914.66	2.9540	0.0888
TA*DA*TG	1	628.351	628.351	0.52782	0.4693
Sbj*TA*DA*TG	98	116666	1190.47		
SG*TA*DA*TG	1	296.461	296.461	0.24903	0.6189
Error	0	0			
Total	799	12771399			

General Results Male Subjects
808 total cases of which 408 are missing
ANOVA
Analysis of Variance for Median <Response Time>
cases selected according to Male Subjects

SOURCE	DF	SUM OF SQ	MEAN SQ	F-RATIO	PROB
Const	1	179048485	179048485	1222.7	<=0.0001
Sbj	49	7175183	146432		
Trt	1	45135.0	45135.0	7.6289	0.0081
Sbj*Trt	49	289900	5916.33		
TG	1	156.250	156.250	0.07058	0.7916
Sbj*TGr	49	108470	2213.67		
Trt*TGr	1	10030.0	10030.0	7.8097	0.0074
Sbj*Trt*TGr	49	62931.0	1284.31		
Dsr	1	86.4900	86.4900	0.05201	0.8206
Sbj*Dsr	49	81491.1	1663.08		
Trt*Dsr	1	3108.06	3108.06	3.5296	0.0662
Sbj*Trt*Dsr	49	43147.7	880.565		
TGr*Dsr	1	3708.81	3708.81	2.5974	0.1135
Sbj*TGr*Dsr	49	69966.3	1427.88		
Trt*TGr*Dsr	1	792.423	792.422	0.40606	0.5269
Sbj*Trt*TGr*Dsr	49	95623.6	1951.50		
Error	0	0			
Total	399	7989730			

GENERAL RESULTS
Female Subjects only
800 total cases of which 400 are missing
ANOVA
Analysis of Variance for Median <Response Time>
Selector Female

SOURCE	DF	SUMS OF SQ	MEAN SQ	F-RATIO	PROB
Const	1	179821395	179821385	2166.9	<=0.0001
Sbj	49	4066384	82987.4		
Trt	1	38220.2	38220.2	7.8156	0.0074
Sbj*Trt	49	239623	4890.26		
Dsr	1	2824.92	2824.92	2.9275	0.0934
Sbj*Dsr	49	47283.3	964.965		
Trt*Dsr	1	1218.01	1218.01	1.3902	0.2441
Sbj*Trt*Dsr	49	42930.7	876.136		
Tgr	1	107.123	107.122	0.08534	0.7714
Sbj*Tgr	49	61410.3	1255.31		
Trt*TGr	1	20363.3	20363.3	11.572	0.0013
Sbj*Trt*TGr	49	86223.6	1759.67		
Dsr*TGr	1	264.063	264.062	0.43835	0.5110
Sbj*Dsr*TGr	49	29517.9	602.406		
Trt*Dsr*TGr	1	116.640	116.640	0.18227	0.6713
Sbj*Trt*Dsr*TGr	49	31356.5	639.930		
Error	0	0			
Total	399	4667943			

GENERAL RESULTS
280 Total cases
ANOVA
Analysis of Variance for Proportion Correct
No Selector
Results are for all data without regard for subject gender

SOURCE	DF	SUMS OF SQ	MEAN SQ	F-RATIO	PROB
Const	1	257.592	257.592	72696	<=0.0001
SN	69	0.244496	0.0003543		
Aft	1	0.000188	0.000188	0.07232	0.7888
SN*Aft	69	0.178958	0.002594		
TG	1	0.001304	0.001304	1.1098	0.2958
SN*TG	69	0.081053	0.001175		
Aft*TG	1	0.001688	0.001688	1.0288	0.3140
SN*Aft*TG	69	0.113221	0.001641		
Error	0	0			
Total	279	0.620907			

GENERAL RESULTS
280 Total cases
ANOVA
Analysis of Variance for Proportion Correct
No Selector

SOURCE	DF	SUMS OF SQ	MEAN SQ	F-RATIO	PROB
Const	1	257.592	257.592	72340	<=0.0001
SN	68	0.242138	0.003561		
SG	1	0.002358	0.002358	0.66212	0.4187
Aft	1	0.000188	0.000188	0.07945	0.7789
SN*Aft	68	0.160541	0.002361		
SG*Aft	1	0.018417	0.018417	7.8007	0.0068
TG	1	0.001304	0.001304	1.1013	0.2977
SN*TG	68	0.080494	0.001184		
SG*TG	1	0.000560	0.000560	0.47272	0.4941
Aft*TG	1	0.001688	0.01688	1.0513	0.3088
SN*Aft*TG	68	0.109189	0.001606		
SG*Aft*TG	1	0.004032	0.004032	2.5109	0.1177
Error	0	0			
Total	279	0.620907			

GENERAL RESULTS
281 Total cases of which 1 is missing
ANOVA
Analysis of Variance for Median <Response Time>
281 total cases of which 1 is missing

SOURCE	DF	SUMS OF SQ	MEAN SQ	F-RATIO	PROB
Const	1	131276162	131276162	1120.5	<=0.0001
Sbj	68	7966782	117159		
SG	1	77922.3	77922.3	0.66510	0.4176
Aft	1	25613.2	25613.2	13.105	0.0006
Sbj*Aft	68	132901	1954.43		
SG*Aft	1	785.575	785.575	0.40195	0.5282
TG	1	5796.70	5796.70	8.4578	0.0049
Sbj*TG	68	46604.9	685.366		
SG*TG	1	9.28929	9.28929	0.01355	0.9077
Aft*TG	1	2484.13	2484.13	3.3805	0.0703
Sbj*Aft*TG	68	49968.9	734.837		
SG*Aft*TG	1	254.604	254.604	0.34648	0.5581
Error	0	0			
Total	279	8309123			

GENERAL RESULTS
281 Total cases of which 141 are missing
ANOVA
Analysis of Variance for Median <Response Time>
Cases selected according to Female Subject

SOURCE	DF	SUMS OF SQ	MEAN SQ	F-RATIO	PROB
Const	1	68875376	68875376	741.02	<=0.0001
Sbj	34	3160191	92946.8		
Aft	1	8713.72	8713.72	4.6860	0.0375
Sbj*Aft	34	63224.2	1859.54		
TG	1	3135.04	3135.04	6.4186	0.0161
Sbj*TG	34	16606.6	488.431		
*Aft*TG*	*1*	*2164.64*	*2164.64*	*3.9509*	*0.0549**
Sbj*Aft*TG	34	18628.0	547.884		
Error	0	0			
Total	139	3272663			

*This interaction is not even close on the male subjects

GENERAL RESULTS MALE SUBJECTS
281 Total cases of which 141 are missing
ANOVA
Analysis of Variance for Median <Response Time>

SOURCE	DF	SUMS OF. SQ	MEAN SQ	F-RATIO	PROB
Const	1	62478708	62478708	441.95	<=0.0001
Sbj	34	4806592	141370		
Aft	1	17685.0	17685.0	8.6297	0.0059
Sbj*Aft	34	69677.2	2049.33		
TG	1	2670.94	2670.94	3.0272	0.0909
Sbj*TG	34	29998.2	882.301		
Aft*TG	1	574.087	574.087	0.62280	0.4355
Sbj*Aft*TG	34	31340.8	921.790		
Error	0	0			
Total	139	4958538			

Appendix B

SCHEFFE POST HOC TESTS Experiment Ib
for factor
Subject Gender*Target Affect*Distractor Affect*Target Gender
Mean Proportion Correct

	Differences Std.	Error	Prob
S male, T angry, D angry, female —S female, T angry, D angry, female	0.002006	0.0074	0.788015
S female, T happy, D angry, female —S female, T angry, D angry, female	-0.001630	0.0074	0.826987
S female, T happy, D angry, female —S male, T angry, D angry, female	0.003636	0.0074	0.626090
S male, T happy, D angry, female —S female, T angry, D angry, female	-0.005082	0.0074	0.496122
S male, T happy, D angry, female —S male, T angry, D angry, female	-0.007088	0.0074	0.343046
S female, T happy, D angry, female —S female, T happy, D angry female	-0.003452	0.0074	0.643676
S female, T angry, D happy, female —S female, T angry, D angry, female	0.008092	0.0074	0.279401
S female, T angry, D happy, female —S male, T angry, D angry, female	0.006086	0.0074	0.417306
S female, T angry, D happy, female —S female, T happy, D angry, female	0.009722	0.0074	0.194325
S female, T angry, D happy, female —S male, T happy, D angry, female	0.013174	0.0074	0.079696
S male, T angry, D happy, female —S female, T angry, D angry, female	-0.005567	0.0074	0.456037
S male, T angry, D happy, female —S female, T angry, D angry, female	-0.007573	0.0074	0.311193
S male, T angry, D happy, female —S male, T angry, D angry, female	-0.003937	0.0074	0.597861
S male, T angry, D happy, female—S female, T happy, D angry, female	-0.000845	0.0074	0.948145
S male, T angry, D happy, female —S female, T angry, D happy, female	-0.013659	0.0074	0.069383
S female, T happy, D happy, female —S female, T angry, D angry, female	0.006630	0.0074	0.374983
S female, T happy, D happy, female —S male, T angry, D angry, female	0.004625	0.0074	0.535638
S female, T happy, D happy, female —S female, T happy, D angry, female	0.008261	0.0074	0.269546
S female, T happy, D happy, female —S male, T happy, D a ngry, female	0.011713	0.0074	0.118619
S female, T happy, D happy, female —S female, T angry, D Happy, Female	-0.001461	0.0074	0.844667
S female, T happy, D happy, female —S male, T angry, D happy, female	0.012198	0.0074	0.104295
S male, T happy, D happy, female, female—S female, T angry, D angry, female	-0.011851	0.0074	0.114383
S male, T happy, D happy, female —S male, T angry, D angry, female	-0.013857	0.0074	0.065512
S female, T happy, D happy, female —S female, T happy, D angry, female	-0.010221	0.0074	0.172627
S male, T happy, D happy, female —S male, T happy, D angry, female	-0.006769	0.0074	0.365142
S female, T happy, D happy, female —S female, T angry, D happy, femal e	-0.019943	0.0074	0.008621
S male, T happy, D happy, female —S male, T angry. D happy, femal e	-0.006284	0.0074	0.400374
S male, T happy, D happy, female —S female, T happy, D happy, female	-0.018482	0.0074	0.014679
S female, T angry, D angry, male —S female, T angry, D angry, female	0.008287	0.0074	0.268026
S female, T angry, D angry, male —S male, T angry, D angry, female	0.006281	0.0074	0.400546
S female, T angry, D angry, male —S female, T happy, D angry, female	0.009918	0.0074	0.185589
S female, T angry, D angry, male —S male—T happy, D angry, female	0.013370	0.0074	0.075400

	Differences Std.	Error	Prob
S female, T angry, D angry, male —S female -T angry, D happy, female	0.000195	0.0074	0.979104
S female, T angry, D angry, male —S male—T angry, D happy, female	0.013855	0.0074	0.065556
S female, T angry, D angry, male —S female T happy, D happy, female	0.001657	0.0074	0.824227
S female, T angry, D angry, male —S male, T happy, D happy, female	0.020138	0.0074	0.008012
S male, T angry, D angry, male —S female, T angry, D angry, female	-0.006366	0.0074	0.394222
S male, T angry, D angry, male —S male, T angry, D angry, female	-0.008372	0.0074	0.263177
S male, T angry, D angry, male —S female, T happy, D angry, female	-0.004736	0.0074	0.525870
S male, T angry, D angry, male —S male, T happy, D angry, female	-0.001284	0.0074	0.863323
S male, T angry, D angry, male —S female, T angry, D happy, female	-0.014458	0.0074	0.054832
S male, T angry, D angry, male —S male, T angry, D happy, female	-0.000799	0.0074	0.914694
S male, T angry, D angry, male —S female, T happy, D happy, female	-0.012997	0.0074	0.083771
S male, T angry, D angry, male —S male, T happy, D happy, female	0.005485	0.0074	0.462741
S male, T angry, D angry, male —S female, T angry, D angry, male	-0.014654	0.0074	0.051696
S female, T happy, D angry, male —S female, T angry, D angry, female	-0.001963	0.0074	0.792434
S female, T happy, D angry, male —S male, T angry, D angry, female	-0.003969	0.0074	0.594898
S female, T happy, D angry, male —S female, T happy, D angry, female	-0.000333	0.0074	0.964423
S female, T happy, D ang ry, male —S male, T happy, D angry, female	0.003119	0.0074	0.675927
S female, T happy, D angry, male —S female, T angry, D happy, female	-0.010055	0.0074	0.179628
S female, T happy, D angry, male —S male, T angry, D happy, female	0.003604	0.0074	0.629122
S female, T happy, D angry, male —S female, T happy, D happy, female	-0.008594	0.0074	0.250853
S female, T happy, D angry, male —S male, T happy, D happy, female	0.009888	0.0074	0.186896
S female, T happy, D angry, male —S female, T angry, D angry, male	-0.010250	0.0074	0.171397
S female, T happy, D angry, male —S male, T angry, D angry, male	0.004403	0.0074	0.555293
S male, T happy, D angry, male —S female, T angry, D angry, female	0.002671	0.0074	0.720319
S male, T happy, D angry, male —S male, T angry, D a ngry, female	0.000665	0.0074	0.928916
S male, T happy, D angry, male —S female, T happy, D angry, female	0.004302	0.0074	0.564444
S male, T happy, D angry, male —S male, T happy, D angry, female	0.007754	0.0074	0.299875
S male, T happy, D angry, male —S female, T angry, D happy, female	-0.005421	0.0074	0.467969
S male, T happy, D angry, male —S male, T angry, D happy, female	0.008239	0.0074	0.270823
S male, T happy, D angry, male —S female, T happy, D happy, female	-0.003959	0.0074	0.595808
S male, T happy, D angry, male —S male, T happy, D happy, female	0.014522	0.0074	0.052786
S male, T happy, D angry, male —S female, T angry, D angry, male	-0.005616	0.0074	0.452129

	Differences Std.	Error	Prob
S male, T happy, D angry, male —S male, T angry, D angry, male	0.009038	0.0074	0.227355
S male, T happy, D angry, male —S female, T happy, D angry, male	0.004634	0.0074	0.534774
S female, T angry, D happy, male —S female, T an gry, D angry, female	0.008218	0.0074	0.272019
S female, T angry, D happy, male —S male, T angry, D angry, female	0.006212	0.0074	0.405739
S female, T angry, D happy, male —S female, T happy, D angry, female	0.009848	0.0074	0.188650
S female T angry, D hap py, male —S male, T happy, D angry, female	0.013300	0.0074	0.076900
S female, T angry, D happy, male —S female, T angry, D happy, female	0.000126	0.0074	0.986507
S female, T angry, D happy, male —S male, T angry, D happy, female	0.013785	0.0074	0.066891
S female, T angry, D happy, male —S female, T happy, D happy, female	0.001588	0.0074	0.831456
S female, T angry, D happy, male —S male, T happy, D happy, female	0.020069	0.0074	0.008223
S female, T angry, D happy, male —S female, T angry, D angry, male	-0.000069	0.0074	0.992595
S female, T angry, D happy, male —S male, T angry, D angry, male	0.014584	0.0074	0.052789
S female, T angry, D happy, male —S female—T happy, D angry, male	0.010181	0.0074	0.174280
S female, T angry, D happy, male —S male, T happy, D an gry, male	0.005547	0.0074	0.457706
S male, T angry, D happy, male —S female—T angry, D angry, female	-0.012694	0.0074	0.091115
S male, T angry, D happy, male —S male, T angry, D angry, female	-0.014700	0.0074	0.050972
S male, T angry, D happy, male —S female, T happy, D angry, female	-0.011064	0.0074	0.140180
S male, T angry, D happy, male —S male, T happy, D angry, female	-0.007612	0.0074	0.308746
S male, T angry, D happy, male —S female, T angry, D happy, female	-0.020786	0.0074	0.006262
S male, T angry, D happy, male —S male, T angry, D happy, female	-0.007127	0.0074	0.340436
S male, T angry, D happy, male —S female, T happy, D happy, female	-0.019325	0.0074	0.010835
S male, T angry, D happy, male —S male, T happy, D happy, female	-0.000843	0.0074	0.909995
S male, T angry, D happy, male - S female, T angry, D angry, male	-0.020982	0.0074	0.005808
S male, T angry, D happy, male —S male, T angry, D angry, male	-0.006328	0.0074	0.397080
S male, T angry, D happy, male —S female, T happy, D angry, male	-0.010731	0.0074	0.152363
S male, T angry, D happy, male —S male, T happy, D angry, male	-0.015366	0.0074	0.041526
S male, T angry, D happy, male —S female, T angry, D happy, male	-0.020912	0.0074	0.005965
S female, T happy, D happy, male —S female, T angry, D an gry, female	-0.000014	0.0074	0.998545
S female, T happy, D happy, male —S male, T angry, D angry, female	-0.002020	0.0074	0.786613
S female, T happy, D happy, male —S female, T happy, D angry, female	0.001617	0.0074	0.828407
S female, T happy, D happy, ma le—S male, T happy, D angry, female	0.005069	0.0074	0.497272
S female, T happy, D happy, male —S female, T angry, D happy, female	-0.008106	0.0074	0.278598

	Differences Std.	Error	Prob
S female, T happy, D happy, male —S female, T angry, D happy, female	-0.008106	0.0074	0.278598
S female, T happy, D happy, male —S male, T angry, D happy, female	0.005554	0.0074	0.457136
S female, T happy, D happy, male —S female, T happy, D happy, female	-0.006644	0.0074	0.374008
S female, T happy, D happy, male —S male, T happy, D happy, female	0.011838	0.00740	0.114794
S female, T happy, D happy, male —S female, T angry, D angry, male	-0.008301	0.0074	0.267246
S female, T happy, D happy, male —S male, T angry, D angry, male	0.006353	0.0074	0.395229
S female, T happy, D happy, male —S female, T happy, D angry, male	0.001949	0.0074	0.793839
S female, T happy, D happy, male —S male, T happy, D angry, male	-0.002685	0.0074	0.718957
S female, T happy, D happy, male —S female, T angry, D happy, male	-0.008232	0.0074	0.271231
S female, T happy, D happy, male —S male, T angry, D happy, male	0.012681	0.0074	0.091457
S male, T happy, D happy, male —S female, T angry, D angry, female	0.001298	0.0074	0.861877
S male, T happy, D happy, male —S male, T angry, D angry, female	-0.000708	0.0074	0.924364
S male, T happy, D happy, male —S female, T happy, D angry, female	0.002928	0.0074	0.694734
S male, T happy, D happy, male — S male, T happy, D angry, female	0.006380	0.0074	0.393208
S male, T happy, D happy, male — S female, T angry, D happy, female	-0.006794	0.0074	0.363355
S male, T happy, D happy, male — S male, T angry, D happy, female	0.006865	0.0074	0.358378
S male, T happy, D happy, m ale —S female, T happy, D happy, female	-0.005333	0.0074	0.475204
S male, T happy, D happy, male — S male, T happy, D happy, female	0.013149	0.0074	0.080269
S male, T happy, D happy, male — S female, T angry, D angry, male	-0.006989	0.0074	0.349781
S male, T happy, D happy, male — S male, T angry, D angry, male	0.007664	0.0074	0.305454
S male, T happy, D happy, male —S female, T happy, D angry, male	0.003261	0.0074	0.662124
S male, T happy, D happy, male —S male, T happy, D angry, male	-0.001374	0.0074	0.853908
S male, T happy, D happy, male —S female, T angry, D happy, male	-0.006920	0.0074	0.354553
S male, T happy, D happy, male —S male, T angry, D happy, male	0.013992	0.0074	0.062973
S male, T happy, D happy, male —S female, T happy, D happy, male	0.001311	0.0074	0.860445

SCHEFFE POST HOC TESTS ExpII
for factors Subject Gender*Target Affect*Target Gender
Proportion Correct

	Differences Std.	Error	Prob
S male, angry, female —S female, angry, female	-0.000000	0.0096	0.999995
S female, happy, female —S female, angry, female	0.011905	0.0096	0.218208
S female, happy, female —S male, angry, female	0.011905	0.0096	0.218206
S male, happy, female —S female, angry, female	-0.005357	0.0096	0.577823
S male, happy, female —S male, angry, female	-0.005357	0.0096	0.577827
S male, happy, female —S female, happy, female	-0.017262	0.0096	0.075968
S female, angry, male —S female, angry, female	-0.001190	0.0096	0.901470
S female, angry, male —S male, angry, female	-0.001190	0.0096	0.901470
S female, angry, male —S female, happy, female	-0.013095	0.0096	0.176102
S male, angry, male —S male, angry, female	0.004167	0.0096	0.66950
S male, angry, ma le—S female, angry, female	0.019643	0.0096	0.044159
S male, angry, male —S male, angry, female	0.019643	0.0096	0.044158
S male, angry, male —S female, happy, female	0.007738	0.0096	0,422003
S male, angry, male —S male, happy, female	0.025000	0.0096	0.011130
S male, angry, male —S female, angry, male	0.020833	0.0096	0.033118
S female, happy, male —S female, angry, female	0.01607	0.0096	0.97978
S female, happy, male —S male, angry, female	0.016071	0.0096	0.097977
S female, happy, male —S female, happy, female	0.004167	0.0096	0.664948
S female, happy, male —S male, happy, female	0.021429	0.0096	0.029565
S female, happy, male —S female, angry, male	0.017262	0.0096	0.075967
S female, happy, male —S male, angry, male	-0.003571	0.0096	0.710423
S male, happy, male —S female, angry, female	-0.010714	0.0096	0.267277
S male, happy, male —S male, angry, female	-0.010714	0.0096	0.267280
S male, happy, male —S female, happy, female	-0.022619	0.0096	0.021081
S male, happy, male —S male, happy, female	-0.005357	0.0096	0.577815
S male, happy, male —S female, angry, male	-0.009524	0.0096	0.323623
S male, happy, male —S male, angry, male	-0.030357	0.0096	0.002292
S male, happy, male —S female, happy, male	-0.026786	0.0096	0.006714

SCHEFFE POST HOC TESTS Experiment Ib
for factors Subject Gender*Distractor Affect
Mean Proportion Correct

	Differences Std.	Error	Prob
S male, D angry —S female, D angry	-0.002866	0.0035	0.420170
S female, D happy —S female, D angry	-0.004558	0.0035	0.200997
S female, D happy —S male, D angry	0.007425	0.0035	0.038577
S male, D happy —S female, D angry	-0.0083777	0.0035	0.019952
S male, D happy —S male, D angry	-0.005511	0.0035	0.122833
S male, D happy —S female, D happy	-0.012935	0.0035	0.000418

SCHEFFE POST HOC TESTS Experiment Ib
for factors Subject Gender*Target Affect*Target Gender
Mean Proportion Correct

	Differences Std.	Error	Prob
S male, D angry, female —S female, D angry, female	-0.000723	0.0039	0.853463
S female, D happy, female —S female, D angry, female	0.008176	0.0039	0.038820
S female, D happy, female —S male, D angry, female	0.008899	0.0039	0.024811
S male, D happy, female —S female, D angry, female	-0.007894	0.0039	0.045911
S male, D happy, female —S female, D angry, female	-0.007171	0.0039	0.069281
S male, D happy, female —S male, D angry, female	-0.007573	0.0074	0.311193
S male, D hap py, female—S female, D happy, female	-0.016070	0.0039	0.000080
S female, D angry, male —S female, D angry, female	0.003977	0.0039	0.310849
S female, D angry, male —S male, D angry, female	0.004700	0.0039	0.231528
S female, D angry, male —S female, D happ y, female	-0.004199	0.0039	0.284786
S female, D angry, male —S male, D happy, female	0.011871	0.0039	0.003028
S male, D angry, male S female, D angry, female	-0.001032	0.0039	0.792010
S male, D angry, male —S male, D angry, female	-0.000309	0.0039	0.937010
S male, D angry, male —S female, D happy, female	-0.009209	0.0039	0.020327
S male, D angry, male —S male, D happy, female	0.006862	0.0039	0.081956
S male, D angry, male —S female, D angry, male	-0.005010	0.0039	0.202472
S female, D happy, male —S female, D angry, female	0.004917	0.0039	0.210839
S female, D happy, male —S male, D angry, female	0.005640	0.0039	0151733
S female, D happy, male —S female, D happy, female	-0.003259	0.0039	0.405907
S female, D happy, male —S male, D happy, female	0.012812	0.0039	0.001432
S female, D happy, male —S female, D angry, male	0.000940	0.0039	0.810216
S female, D happy, male —S male, D angry, male	0.005950	0.0039	0.130748
S male, D happy, male —S female D angry, female	-0.004883	0.0039	0.214021
S male, D happy, male —S male, D angry, female	-0.004160	0.0039	0. 289262
S male, D happy, male —S female, D happy, female	-0.013059	0.0039	0.001167
S male, D happy, male —S male, D happy, female	0.003011	0.0039	0.442435
S male, D happy, male —S female, D angry, male	-0.008860	0.0039	0.025435
S male, D happy, male —S male, D angry, male	-0.003851	0.0039	0.326424
S male, D happy, male —S female, D happy, male	-0.009800	0.0039	0.013704

SCHEFFE POST HOC TESTS Experiment 1b
for factors
Subject Gender*Target Affect*Distractor Affect*Target Gender
Median <Response Time>

	Differences Std.	Error	Prob
S male, T angry, D angry, female —S female, T angry, D angry, female	-10.1400	6.901	0.144919
S female, T happy, D angry, female —S female, T angry, D angry, female	-35.6300	6.901	0.000001
S female, T happy, D angry, female —S male, T angry, D angry, female	-25.4900	6.901	0.000364
S male, T happy, D angry, female —S female, T angry, D angry, female	-10.8700	6.901	0.118429
S male, T happy, D angry, female —S male, T angry, D angry, female	-0.730000	6.901	0.915967
S male, T happy, D angry, female —S female, T happy, D angry female	24.7600	6.901	0.000522
S female, T angry, D happy, female —S female, T angry, D angry, female	3.06000	6.901	0.658427
S female, T angry, D happy, female —S male, T angry, D angry, female	13.2000	6.901	0.058684
S female, T angry, D happy, female —S female, T happy, D angry, female	38.6900	6.901	0.000000
S female, T angry, D happy, female —S male, T happy, D angry, female	13.9300	6.901	0.046255
S male, T angry, D happy, female —S female, T angry, D angry, fem ale	-8.85000	6.901	0.202696
S male, T angry, D happy, female —S male, T angry, D angry, female	1.29000	6.901	0.852095
S male, T angry, D happy, female —S female, T happy, D angry, female	26.7800	6.901	0.000189
S male, T angry, D happy, female —S male, T ha ppy, D angry, female	2.02000	6.901	0.770350
S male, T angry, D happy, female —S female, T angry, D happy, female	-11.9100	6.901	0.087512
S female, T happy, D happy, female —S female, T angry, D happy, female	-28.1300	6..901	0.000093
S female, T happy, D h appy, female —S male, T angry, D angry, female	-17.9900	6.901	0.010560
S female, T happy, D happy, female —S female, T happy, D angry, female	7.50000	6.901	0.279766
S female, T happy, D happy, female —S male, T happy, D angry, female	-17.2600	6.901	0.014034
S female, T happy, D happy, female —S female, T angry, D happy, female	-31.1900	6.901	0.000017
S female, T happy, D happy, female —S male, T angry, D happy, female	-19.2800	6.901	0.006264
S male, T happy, D happy, female —S female, T angry, D angry, femal e	-27.9300	6.901	0.000103
S male, T happy, D happy, female —S male, T angry, D angry, female	-17.7900	6.901	0.011425
S male, T happy, D happy, female —S female, T happy, D angry, female	7.70000	6.901	0.267219
S male, T happy, D happy, female —S male, T happy, D angry, female	-17.0600	6.901	0.015150
S male, T happy, D happy, female —S female, T angry, D happy, female	-30.9900	6.901	0.000019
S male, T happy, D happy, female —S male, T angry, D happy, female	-19.0800	6.901	0.006803
S male, T happy, D happy, female —S female, T happy, D happy, female	0.200000	6.901	0.976937
S female, T angry, D angry, male —S female, T angry, D angry, female	-14.7900	6.901	0.034566
S female, T angry, D angry, male —S male, T angry, D angry, female	-4.65000	6.901	0.501992
S female, T angry, D angry, male —S female, T happy, D angry, female	20.8400	6.901	0.003223

Differences Std.	Error	Prob
S female, T angry, D angry, male —S male—T happy, D angry, female	-3.92000	6.901	0.571291
S female, T angry, D angry, male —S female -T angry, D happy, female	-17.85000	6.901	0.011159
S female, T angry, D angry, male —S male—T angry, D happy, female	-5.94000	6.901	0.391454
S female, T angry, D angry, male —S female T happy, D happy, female	13.3400	6.901	0.056103
S female, T angry, D angry, male —S male, T happy, D happy, female	13.1400	6.901	0.059821
S male, T angry, D angry, m ale—S female, T angry, D angry, female	-3.86000	6.901	0.577186
S male, T angry, D angry, male —S male, T angry, D angry, female	6.28000	6.901	0.365023
S male, T angry, D angry, male —S female, T happy, D angry, female	31.7700	6.901	0.000012
S male, T angry, D angry, male —S female, T happy, D angry, female	7.01000	6.901	0.312203
S male, T angry, D angry, male —S female, T angry, D happy, female	-6.92000	6.901	0.318424
S male, T angry, D angry, male —S male, T angry, D happy, female	4.99000	6.901	0.471327
S male, T angry, D angry, male —S female, T happy, D happy, female	24.2700	6.901	0.000663
S male, T angry, D angry, male —S male, T happy, D happy, female	24.0700	6.901	0.000730
S male, T angry, D angry, male —S female, T angry, D angry, male	10.9300	6.901	0.116535
S female, T happy, D angry, male —S female, T angry, D angry, female	-21.6100	6.901	0.002292
S female, T happy, D angry, male —S male, T angry, D angry, female	-11.4700	6.901	0.099675
S female, T happy, D angry, male —S female, T happy, D angry, fe male	14.0200	6.901	0.044891
S female, T happy, D angry, male —S male, T happy, D angry, female	-10.7400	6.901	0.122842
S female, T happy, D angry, male —S female, T angry, D happy, female	-24.6700	6.901	0.000546
S female, T happy, D angry, male —S male, T angry, D happy, female	-12.7600	6.901	0.067457
S female, T happy, D angry, male —S female, T happy, D happy, female	6.52000	6.901	0.347064
S female, T happy, D angry, male —S male, T happy, D happy, female	6.32000	6.901	0.361989
S female, T happy, D angry, male , —S female, T angry, D angry, male	-6.82000	6.901	0.325432
S female, T happy, D angry, male —S male, T angry, D angry, male	-17.7500	6.901	0.011605
S male, T happy, D angry, male —S female, T angry, D angry, female	-33.1800	6.901	0.000006
S male, T happy, D angry, male —S female, T happy, D angry, female	-23.0400	6.901	0.001191
S male, T happy, D angry, male —S male, T angry, D angry, female	2.45000	6.901	0.723323
S male, T happy, D angry, male —S female, T happy, D angry, female	-22.3100	6.901	0.001669
S male, T happy, D angry, male —S female, T angry, D happy, female	-36.2400	6.901	0.000001
S male, T happy, D angry, male —S male, T angry, D happy, female	-24.3300	6.901	0.000644
S male, T happy, D angry, male —S female, T happy, D happy, female	-5.05000	6.901	0.466027

	Differences Std.	Error	Prob
S male, T happy, D angry, male —S male, T happy, D happy, female	-5.25000	6.910	0.448603
S male, T happy, D angry, male —S female, T angry, D angry, male	-18.3900	6.901	0.009005
S male, T happy, D angry, male —S male, T angry, D angry, male	-29.3200	6.901	0.000049
S male, T happy, D angry, male —S female, T happy, D angry, male	-11.5700	6.901	0.096797
S female, T angry, D happy, male —S female, T angry, D angry, female	-13.6100	6.901	0.051396
S female, T angry, D happy, male —S male, T angry, D angry, female	-3.47000	6.901	0.616196
S female, T angry, D happy, male —S female, T happy, D angry, female	22.0200	6.901	0.001905
S female T angry, D happy, male —S male, T happy, D angry, female	-2.74000	6.901	0.692183
S female, T angry, D happy, male —S female, T angry, D happy, female	-16.6700	6.901	0.017557
S female, T angry, D happy, male —S male, T angry, D happy, female	-4.76000	6.901	0.491955
S female, T angry, D happy, male —S female, T happy, D happy, female	14.5200	6.901	0.037924
S female, T angry, D happy, male —S male, T happy, D happy, female	14.3200	6.901	0.040590
S female, T angry, D happy, male —S female, T angry, D angry, male	1.18000	6.901	0.864577
S female, T angry, D happy, male —S male, T angry, D angry, male	-9.75000	6.901	0.160849
S female, T angry, D happy, male —S female—T happy, D angry, male	8.00000	6.901	0.249145
S female, T angry, D happy, male —S male, T happy, D angry, male	19.5700	6.901	0.005551
S male, T angry, D happy, male —S female—T angry, D angry, female	5.95000	6.901	0.390660
S male, T angry, D happy, male —S male, T angry, D angry, female	16.0900	6.901	0.021765
S male, T angry, D happy, male —S female, T happy, D angry, female	41.5800	6.901	0.000000
S male, T angry, D happy, male —S male, T happy, D ang ry, female	16.8200	6.901	0.016593
S male, T angry, D happy, male —S female, T angry, D happy, female	2.89000	6.901	0.676277
S male, T angry, D happy, male —S male, T angry, D happy, female	14.8000	6.901	0.034447
S male, T angry, D happy, male —S female, T happy, D happy, female	34.0800	6.901	0.000003
S male, T angry, D happy, male —S male, T happy, D happy, female	33.8800	6.901	0.000004
S male, T angry, D happy, male - S female, T angry, D angry, male	20.7400	6.901	0.003367
S male, T angry, D happy, male —S male, T angry, D angry, male	9.81000	6.901	0.158314
S male, T angry, D happy, male —S female, T happy, D angry, male	27.5600	6.901	0.000126
S male, T angry, D happy, male —S male, T happy, D angry, male	39.1300	6.901	0.000000
S male, T angry, D happy, m ale—S female, T happy, D happy, male	19.5600	6.901	0.005574
S female, T happy, D happy, male —S female, T angry, D angry, male	-13.7700	6.901	0.048768
S female, T happy, D happy, male —S male, T angry, D angry, female	-3.63000	6.901	0.600050

	Differences Std.	Error	Prob
S female, T happy, D happy, male —S female, T happy, D angry, female	21.8600	6.901	0.002048
S female, T happy, D happy, male —S male, T happy, D angry, female	-2.90000	6.901	0.675222
S female, T happy, D happy, male —S female, T angry, D happy, female	-16.8300	6.901	0.016531
S female, T happy, D happy, male —S male, T angry, D happy, female	-4.92000	6.901	0.477553
S female, T happy, D happy, male —S female, T happy, D happy, female	14.3600	6.901	0.040044
S female, T happy, D ha ppy, male —S male, T happy, D happy, female	14.1600	6.901	0.042838
S female, T happy, D happy, male —S female, T angry, D angry, male	1.02000	6.901	0.882794
S female, T happy, D happy, male —S male, T angry, D angry, male	-9.91000	6.901	0.154158
S female, T happy, D happy, male —S female, T happy, D angry, male	7.84000	6.901	0.258674
S female, T happy, D happy, male —S male, T happy, D angry, male	19.4100	6.901	0.005934
S female, T happy, D happy, male —S female, T angry, D happy, male	-0.16000	6.901	0.981549
S female, T happy, D happy, male —S male, T angry, D happy, male	-19.7200	6.901	0.005212
S male, T happy, D happy, male —S female, T angry, D angry, female	-29.7600	6.901	0.000038
S male, T happy, D happy, male —S male, T angry, D angry, female	-19.6200	6.901	0.005436
S male, T happy, D happy, male —S female, T happy, D angry, female	5.87000	6.901	0.397039
S male, T happy, D happy, male —S male, T happy, D angry, female	-18.8900	6.901	0.007354
S male, T happy, D happy, male —S female, T angry, D happy, female	-32.8200	6.901	0.000007
S male, T happy, D happy, male —S male, T angry, D happy, female	-20.9100	6.901	0.003126
S male, T happy, D happy, male —S female, T happy, D happy, female	-1.63000	6.901	0.813762
S male, T happy, D happy, male —S male, T happy, D happy, female	-1.83000	6.901	0.791418
S male, T happy, D happy, male —S female, T angry, D angry, male	-14.9700	6.901	0.032473
S male, T happy, D happy, male —S male, T angry, D angry, male	-25.9900	6.901	0.000296
S male, T happy, D happy, male —S female, T happy, D angry, male	-8.15000	6.901	0.240441
S male, T happy, D happy, male —S male, T happy, D angry, male	3.42000	6.901	0.621281
S male, T happy, D happy, male —S female, T angry, D happy, male	-16.1500	6.901	0.021292
S male, T happy, D happy , male—S male, T angry, D happy, male	-35.7100	6.901	0.000001
S male, T happy, D happy, male —S female, T happy, D happy, male	-15.9900	6.901	0.022575

SCHEFFE POST HOC TESTS ExpII
for factors Subject Gender*Target Affect*Target Gender
Median <Response Time>

	Differences Std.	Error	Prob
S male, angry, female —S female, angry, female	-32.2857	6.480	0.000005
S female, happy, female —S female, angry, female	-23.6429	6.480	0.000512
S female, happy, female —S male, angry, female	8.64286	6.480	0.186730
S male, happy, female—S female, angry, female	-58.8143	6.480	0.000000
S male, happy, female —S male, angry, female	-26.5286	6.480	0.000115
S male, happy, female —S female, happy, female	-35.1714	6.480	0.000001
S female, angry, male —S female, angry, female	-17.3286	6.480	0.009374
S female, angry, male —S male, angry, female	14.9571	6.480	0.024036
S female, angry, male —S female, happy, female	6.31429	6.480	0.333300
S female, angry, male —S male, happy, female	41.4857	6.480	0.000000
S male, angry, male —S female, angry, female	-45.0714	6.480	0.000000
S male, angry, male —S male, angry, female	-12.7857	6.480	0.052551
S male, angry, male —S female, happy, female	-21.4286	6.480	0.001510
S male, angry, male —S male, happy, female	13.7429	6.480	0.037588
S male, angry, male —S female, angry, male	-27.7429	6.480	0.000060
S female, happy, male —S female, angry, female	-25.2429	6.480	0.000226
S female, happy, male —S male, angry, female	7.04286	6.480	0.280938
S female, happy, male —S female, happy, female	-1.60000	6.480	0.805720
S female, happy, male —S male, happy, female	33.5714	6.480	0.000002
S female, happy, male —S female, angry, male	-7.91429	6.480	0.226176
S female, happy, male —S male, angry, male	19.8286	6.480	0.003167
S male, happy, male —S female, angry, female	-63.5000	6.480	0.000000
S male, happy, male —S male, angry, female	-31.2143	6.480	0.000009
S male, happy, male —S female, happy, female	-39.8571	6.480	0.000000
S male, happy, male —S male, happy, female	-4.68571	6.480	0.472097
S male, happy, male —S female, angry, male	-46.1714	6.480	0.000000
S male, happy, male —S male, angry, male	-18.4286	6.480	0.005881
S male, happy, male —S female, happy, male	038.2571	6.480	0.000000

SCHEFFE POST HOC TESTS ExpII
for factors Target Affect*Target Gender—Proportion Correct

	Differences Std.	Error	Prb
happy, female—angry, female	0.003274	0.0068	0.634064
angry, male—angry, female	0.009226	0.0068	0.182235
angry, male—happy, female	0.005952	0.0068	0.387675
happy, male—angry, female	0.002679	0.0068	0.696852
happy, male—happy, female	-0.000595	0.0068	0.930976
happy, male—angry, male	-0.006548	0.0068	0.342273

SCHEFFE POST HOC TESTS Experiment Ib
for factors
Target Affect*Target Gender*Distractor Affect
Median <Response Time>

	Differences Std.	Error	Prob
happy, female, angry —angry, female, angry	-2.84000	8.835	0.749242
angry, male, angry —angry, female, angry	5.4900	8.835	0.537229
angry, male, angry —happy, female, angry	8.33000	8.835	0.350397
happy, male, angry —angry, female, angry	-23.0100	8.835	0.012151
happy, male, angry —happy, female, angry	-20.1700	8.835	0.026811
happy, male, angry —angry, male, angry	-28.5000	8.835	0.002240
angry, female, happy —angry, female angry	1.37000	8.835	0.877409
angry, female, happy —happy, female, angry	4.21000	8.835	0.635833
angry, female, happy —angry, male, angry	-4.12000	8.835	0.643054
angry, female, happy —happy, male angry	24.8300	8.835	0.008120
happy, female, happy —angry, female, angry	-18.2500	8.835	0.044175
happy, female, happy —happy, female, angry	-15.4100	8.835	0.087401
happy, female, happy —angry, male, angry	-23.7400	8.835	0.009819
happy, female, happy —happy, male, angry	4.76000	8.835	0.592494
happy, female, happy —angry, female, happy	-19.6200	8.835	0.031028
angry, male, happy—angry, female, angry	13.4100	8.835	0.135491
angry, male, happy —happy female, angry	16.2500	8.835	0.071943
angry, male, happy —angry, male, angry	7.92000	8.835	0.374412
angry, male, happy —happy, male, angry	36.4200	8.835	0.000144
angry, male, happy —angry female, happy	12.0400	8.835	0.179196
angry, male, happy —happy, female, happy	31.6600	8.835	0.000779
happy, male, happy —angry, female, angry	-20.6100	8.835	0.023813
happy, male, happy —happy, female, angry	-17.7700	8.835	0.049813
happy, male, happy —angry, male, angry	-26.1000	8.835	0.004807
happy, male, happy —happy, male, angry	2.40000	8.835	0.787039
happy, male, happy —angry, female, happy	-21.9800	8.835	0.016305
happy, male, happy —happy, female, happy	-2.36000	8.835	0.790502
happy, male, happy —angry, male, happy	-34.0200	8.835	0.000342

SCHEFFE POST HOC TESTS Experiment Ib
for factors
Target Affect*Distractor Affect*Target Gender
Median <Response Time>

	Differences Std.	Error	Prob
happy, angry, female —angry, angry, female	-36.2300	5.059	0.000000
angry, happy, female —angry, angry, female	4.53000	5.059	0.374967
angry, happy, female —happy, angry, female	40.7600	5.059	0.000000
happy, happy, female —angry, angry, female	-26.8800	5.059	0.000003
happy, happy, female —happy, angry, female	9.35000	5.059	0.070634
happy, happy, female —angry, happy, female	-31.4100	5.059	0.000000
angry, angry, male —angry, angry, female	-12.6000	5.059	0.016198
angry, angry, male —happy, angry, female	23.6300	5.059	0.000024
angry, angry, male —angry, happy, female	-17.1300	5.059	0.001406
angry, angry, male —happy, happy, female	14.2800	5.059	0.006867
happy, angry, male —angry, angry, female	-22.4500	5.059	0.000052
happy, angry, ma le—happy, angry, female	13.7800	5.059	0.008922
happy, angry, male —angry, happy, female	-26.9800	5.059	0.000002
happy, angry, male —happy, happy, female	4.43000	5.059	0.385518
happy, angry, male —angry, angry, male	-9.85000	5.059	0.057293
angry, happy, ma le—angry, angry, female	-13.4800	5.059	0.010413
angry, happy, male —happy, angry, female	22.7500	5.059	0.000042
angry, happy, male —angry, happy, female	-18.0100	5.059	0.000837
angry, happy, male —happy, happy, female	13.4000	5.059	0.010847
angry, happy, male—angry, angry, male	-0.880000	5.059	0.862633
angry, happy, male —happy, angry, male	8.97000	5.095	0.082453
happy, happy, male —angry, angry, female	-14.1900	5.059	0.007201
happy, happy, male —happy, angry, female	22.0400	5.059	0.000067
happy, happy, m ale—angry, happy, female	-18.7200	5.059	0.000546
happy, happy, male —happy, happy, female	12.6900	5.059	0.015494
happy, happy, male —angry, angry, male	-1.59000	5.059	0.754651
happy, happy, male —happy, angry, male	8.26000	5.059	0.108960
happy, happy, mal e—angry, happy, male	-0.710000	5.059	0.888972

SCHEFFE POST HOC TESTS ExpII
FEMALE—for factors Target Affect*Target Gender
Median <Response Time>

	Differences Std.	*Error*	*Prob*
happy, female—angry, female	-23.6429	5.595	0.000169
angry, male—angry, female	-17.3286	5.595	0/003904
angry, male—happy, female	6.31429	5.595	0.267012
happy, male—angry, female	-25.2429	5.595	0.000073
happy, male—happy, female	-1.60000	5.595	0.776649
happy, male—angry, male	-7.91429	5.595	0.166324

SCHEFFE POST HOC TESTS ExpII
MALE—for factors Target Affect*Target Gender
Median <Response Time>

	Differences Std.	*Error*	*Prob*
happy, female—angry, female	-26.5286	7.258	0.000859
angry, male—angry, female	-12.7857	7.258	0.087113
angry, male—happy, female	13.7429	7.258	0.066818
happy, male—angry, female	-31.2143	7.258	0.000136
happy, male—happy, female	-4.68571	7.258	0.522857
happy, male—angry, male	-18.4286	7.258	0.015854

Appendix C

SUMMARY TABLE I

gender	ta	da	Means	Numeric	stdDevs
female	angry	angry	729.35107	2424	261.38026
female	angry	happy	728.75289	2424	244.96500
female	happy	angry	706.11221	2424	250.99449
female	happy	happy	699.29827	2424	239.22225
male	angry	angry	727.86634	2424	260.80833
male	angry	happy	728.0394	2424	263.22160
male	happy	angry	702.22772	2424	233.95557
male	happy	happy	705.95957	2424	244.92233

SUMMARY TABLE II

subject gender	ta	da	Gender	means	stdDevs
female	angry	angry	Female	727.56454	238.59284
female	angry	angry	Male	713.77042	222.60745
female	angry	happy	Female	734.11111	232.85505
female	angry	happy	Male	717.43873	237.67360
female	happy	angry	Female	697.99673	245.31409
female	happy	angry	Male	706.20915	229.48045
female	happy	happy	Female	690.56454	210.94644
female	happy	happy	Male	703.35212	224.21091
male	angry	angry	Female	731.17333	282.82714
male	angry	angry	Male	742.24417	294.11654
male	angry	happy	Female	723.28750	256.71170
male	angry	happy	Male	738.83500	286.64448
male	happy	angry	Female	714.39000	256.49682
male	happy	angry	Male	698.16667	238.46094
male	happy	happy	Female	708.20667	264.76668
male	happy	happy	Male	708.61917	264.45012

References

Arnoff, A., Woike, B. A., Hyman, L. M., (1992) Which Are the Stimuli in Facial Displays of Anger and Happiness? Configurational Bases of Emotion Recognition *Journal of Personality and Social Psychology* 62 (6), 1050-1066.

Atkinson, R. C., & Shiffrin, R. M., (1968) Human memory: A proposed system and its control processes. In K. W. Spence & J. T. Spence (Eds.), *The psychology of learning and motivation.* New York: Academic Press.

Bargh, J. A., (1982). Attention and automaticity in the processing of self-relevant information. *Journal of Personality and Social Psychology,* 43, 425-436.

Bargh, J. A., (1984) Automatic and conscious processing of social information. In R. S. Wyer, Jr., and T. K. Srull (Eds.), *Handbook of social cognition* (Vol. 3, pp 1-43, Hillsdale, NJ: Erlbaum.

Bargh, J. A., & Pietromonaco, P., (1982). Automatic information processing and social perception: The influence of trait information presented outside of conscious awareness on impression formation. *Journal of Personality and Social Psychology.* 43, 437-449.

Barrera, M. E., & Maurer, D., (1981). The perception of Facial Expressions by the three month old. *Child Development,* 52, 203-206.Benbow, C. P. , & Stanley, J. C., (1980). Sex differences in mathematical ability: fact or artifact. *Science, 210,* 1262-1264.

Bergen, J. R., & Julesz, B., (1983). Parallel versus serial processing in rapid pattern discrimination. *Nature.* 030, 696-698.

Bradshaw, J. L., & Nettleton, N. C., (1983). *Human cerebral asymmetry.* Englewood Cliffs, N. J. : Prentice-Hall.

Broverman, I. K., Vogel, S. R., Broverman, D. M., Clarkson, F. E., & Rosenkrantz, F. E., & Rosenkrantz, P. S., (1972). Sex-role stereotypes: A current appraisal. *Journal of Social Issues,* 28 59-78.

Bruce, V., (1988). *Recognizing Faces.* London: Lawrence Erlbaum Associates, Publishers.

Bruce, V. , Doyle, T., Dench, N., Burton, M,. (1991) Remembering facial configurations. *Journal of Cognition.* Nottingham, England. Vol. 38(2) 109-144.

Buck, R. A., (1979). Measuring individual differences in the nonverbal communication of affect: The slide-viewing paradigm. *Human Communication Research,* 6, 47-57.

Buck, R., Miller, R. E., Caul, W. F., (1974). Sex, personality, and physiological variables in the communication of affect via facial expression. *Journal of Personality and Social Psychology* 30, 587-596.

Johns Hopkins University Press, in press.

Buck, R. W., Savin, V. J., Miller, R. E., & Caul, W. F.,(1972) Communication of Affect Through Facial Expressions in Humans, *Journal of Personality and Social Psychology,* 23(3) 362-371.

Burton, L. A., & Levy, J., (1989) Sex Differences in the Lateralized Processing of Facial Emotion. *Brain and Cognition. 11, 210-228.*

Cheesman, J., & Merikle, P. M., (1986). Distinguishing conscious from unconscious perceptual processes. *Canadian Journal of Psychology,* 40, 343-367.

Cheng, P. W., (1985). Restructuring versus automaticity: Alternative accounts of skill acquisition. *Psychological Review;* 92, 414-423.

Conrad, R., (1964) Acoustic confusions in immediate memory. *British Journal of Psychology,* 55, 75-84.

Darwin, C., (1904) *The expression of emotions in man and animals.* London: Murray. (Original work published in 1872).

Davitz, J. R., (1964). A review of research concerned with facial and vocal expressions of emotion. In J. R. Davitz (Ed.), *The communication of emotional meaning.* New York: McGraw-Hill.

Ekman, P., (1972). Universals and cultural differences in facial expressions of emotion. In J. Cole (Ed.). *Nebraska symposium on motivation.* 1971 (pp. 207-283). Lincoln: University of Nebraska Press.

Ekman, P., (1973). (Ed) *Darwin and Facial Expression: A Century of Research in Review.* New York: Academic Press.

Ekman, P., (Ed.) (1982). Emotion in the human face. New York: Cambridge University Press.

Ekman, P., & Freisen, W. V., (1974) Detecting Deception From the Body or Face. *Journal of Personality and Social Psychology.* 29(3), 288-298.

Ekman, P., & Friesen W. V., (1978a). *Manual for the Facial Action Coding System.* Palo Alto, California: Consulting Psychologists Press.

Ekman, P., & Freisen, W. V., (1978b). *Investigators Guide to the Facial Action Coding System,* part I and II. Palo Alto, California: Consulting Psychologist Press.

Ekman, P., Friesen, W. V., & Ellsworth, P., (1971). *Emotion In The Human Face: Guidelines For Research and a Review of Findings.* New York: Pergamon Press.

Ekman, P., Friesen, W. V., & Ellsworth, P., (1972). *Emotion in the human face.* New York: Pergamon.

Ekman, P, Friesen, W. V., & Ellsworth, P., (1982a) What emotion categories or dimensions can observers judge from facial behaviour? In P. Ekman (Ed.), *Emotion in the human face* (Second Edition). Cambridge: Cambridge University Press.

Ekman, P., & O'Sullivan, M., (1988). The role of context in interpreting facial expression: Comment on Russell and Fehr. *Journal of Experimental Psychology: General,* 117, 86-88.

Erwin, R. J.; Gur, R. C.; Gur, R. E.; Skolnick, B.; Mawhinney-hee, M.; Smailis, J., (1992). Facial Emotion Discrimination: I. Task Construction and Behavioral Findings in Normal Subjects. *Psychiatry Research,* 42, 231-240.

Friesen, W. V. , (1972). *Cultural differences in facial expressions in a social situation: An experimental test of the concept of display rules.* Unpublished doctoral dissertation, University of California, San Francisco.

Gitter, A. G.; Black, H.; & Mostofsky, D., (1972) Race and sex in the perception of emotion. *Journal of Social Issues, 28(4), 63-78 (b).*

Graham, N., (1980) Spatial-Frequency Channels in Human Vision: Detecting Edges Without Edge Detectors. In C. S. Harris (Ed.), *Visual coding and adaptability.* Hillsdale, NJ Lawrence Erlbaum Associates.

Hall, J. A., (1978). Gender Effects in Decoding Nonverbal Cues. *Psychological Bulletin* 85(4) 845-857.

Hall, J. A., (1984). *Nonverbal sex differences: Communication accuracy and expressive style.* Baltimore, MD: Johns Hopkins University Press.

Hansen, C., & Hansen, R., (1987, 1988) Finding the Face in the Crowd: An Anger Superiority Effect. *Journal of Personality and Social Psychology,* 54 (6), 917-924

Harrison, D. W., Gorelczenko, P. M. , & Cook, J., (1990). Sex Differences in the functional asymmetry for facial affect perception. *Intern. J. Neurosciences. 52,* 11-16.

Harper, R. G., Wiens, A. N., & Matarazzo., (1978). *Nonverbal Communication: The State of the Art.* New York: John Wiley & Sons.

Haviland, J. M., & Ingate, M., (1980). Hemispheric differences in the perception of facial expression. Unpublished manuscript.

Hillger, L. A., Koenig, O., (1991). Separable Mechanisms in Face Processing: Evidence from Hemispheric Specialization. *Journal of Cognitive Neuroscience.* 3(1) 42-58.

Hugdahl, K., Iversen, P. M., & Johnsen, B. H., (1993) Laterality For Facial Expressions: Does the Sex of the Subject Interact with the Sex of the Stimulus Face? Cortex. 29, 325-331.

Izard, C., (1971). *The face of emotion,* New York: Appleton-Century Crofts.

Kahneman, D., & Treisman, A., (1983). Changing views of attention and automaticity. In M. Kubovy & J. R. Pomerantz (Eds.), *Varieties of attention.* New York: Academic Press.

Keen, P. G. W. , (1986). Competing in time: Using telecommunications for competitive advantage. Cambridge, MA: Ballinger.

Kirouac, G., & Dorè, F. Y., (1985).Accuracy of the Judgment of Facial Expression of Emotions as a Function of Sex and Level of Education. *Journal of Nonverbal Behavior.* 9(1) 3-7.

Kulikowski, J. J. & King-Smith, P. E., (1973) Spatial arrangements of line, edge, and grating detectors revealed by subthreshold summation. *Vision Research.* 13, 1455-1478.

LaBarbera, J. D., Izard, C. E., Veitze, P., & Parisi, S. A.,(1976) Four-and six-month-old infants' visual responses to joy, anger, and neutral expressions. *Child Development*, 47, 535-538.

Landis, T., Assol, G., & Perret, E., (1979) Opposite cerebral hemisphere superiorities for visual associative processing of emotional facial expression and objects. *Nature (London),*179 739-740.

Logan, G. D., (1979). On the use of a concurrent memory load to measure attention and automaticity. *Journal of Experimental Psychology: Human Perception and Performance,* 5, 189-207.

McGlone, J., (1980). Sex differences in human brain asymmetry: A critical survey. *The Brain and Behavioral Sciences. 3,* 215-227.

Notarius, C. I., Wemple, L. J., Ingraham, Burns, T. J., & Kollar, E., (1982). Multichannel Responses to an Interpersonal Stressor: Interrelationships Among Facial Display, Heart Rate, Self-Report of Emotion and Threat Appraisal. *Journal of Personality and Social Psychology,* 43(3), 400-408.

Purcell, D. G., & Stewart, A. L., (1986). The face-detection effect. *Bulletin of the Psychonomic Society,* 24, 118-120.

Rosenthal, R., Hall, J. A. , DiMatteo, M. R. Roger, P. L., & Archer, D., (1979) *Sensitivity to nonverbal communication: The PONS Test.* Baltimore, MD,

Rotter, N. G., & Rotter, G. S., (1988). Sex Differences in the Encoding and Decoding of Negative Facial Emotions. *Journal of Nonverbal Behavior* 12(2) 139—148.

Safer, M. A., & Leventhal, H., (1977). Ear differences in evaluating emotional tones of voice and verbal content. *Journal of Experimental Psychology: Human Perception and Performance*, 3, 75-82.

Sagi, D., & Julesz, B., (1985a). Detection versus discrimination of visual orientation. *Perception.* 14, 619-629.

Sagi, D., & Julesz, B., (1985b). "Where" and "what" of vision. *Science.* 288, 1217-1219.

Schneider, W. & Shiffrin, R. M., (1977). Controlled and automatic human information processing: I. Detection, search, and attention. *Psychological Review*, 84 1-66.

Schwartz, G. M., Izard, C. E., & Ansul, S. E., (1985). The five-month-old's ability to discriminate facial expressions of emotion. *Infant Behavior and Development*, 8, 65-77.

Shapley, R. M., & Tolhurst, D. J., (1973). Edge detectors in human vision. *Journal Physiology*, London, 229, 165-183.

Shiffrin, R. M., & Atkinson, R. C., (1969) Storage and retrieval processes in long-term memory. *Psychological Review*, 76 179-193.

Shiffrin, R. M., & Schneider, W., (1977). Controlled and automatic human information processing: II Detection, search, and attention. *Psychological Review*, 84, 127-190.

Sperling, G., (1960) The Information Available In Brief Visual Presentations, *Science*, 74(11) 1-26

Springer, S. P., & Deutsch, G., (1989). *Left brain, right brain* 3rd Edition). Sand Francisco: W. H. Freeman.

Stanners, R. F., Byrd, D. M., & Gabriel, R., (1985) The Time It Takes To Identify Facial Expressions: Effects Of Age, Gender of Subject, Sex of Sender, and Type Of Expression. *Journal of Nonverbal Behavior* 9(4), Winter 201-211

Strauss, E., & Moscovitch, M., (1981) Perceptual asymmetries in processing facial expression and facial identity. *Brain and Language*, 13: 308-332.

Tagiuri, R., (1969) Person perception. In G. Lindzey & Aronson (Eds.), *Handbook of social psychology (2nd edition, Vol. 3)* Reading, Mass.: Addison-Wellsley.

Tassone, A. R., (1992). Searching for Easily Detected Stimuli. A dissertation presented to Stevens Institute of Technology.

Treisman, A., (1982). Perceptual grouping and attention in visual search for features and for objects. *Journal of Experimental Psychology: Human Perception and Performance,* 8, 194-214.

Treisman, A., & Gelade, G., (1980). A feature-integration theory of attention. *Cognitive Psychology.* 12, 97-136.

Treisman, A., & Peterson, R., (1984). Emergent features, attention, and object perception. *Journal of Experimental Psychology: Human Perception and Performance,* 10, 194-214.

Treisman, A., & Souther, J.,(1985) Search asymmetry: A Diagnostic for preattentive processing of separable features. *Journal of Experimental Psychology: General,* 114, 285-310.

Tulving, E., & Thomson, D. M., (1971). Retrieval processes in recognition memory: Effects of associative context. *Journal of Experimental Psychology,* 87, 116-124.

Watson, S. G., (1972). Judgment of Emotion From Facial and Contextual Cue Combinations, *Journal of Personality and Social Psychology,* 24(3), 334-342.

Wilcox, B. M., & Clayton, F. L., (1968). Infant visual fixation on motion pictures of the human face. *Journal of Experimental Child Psychology,* 6, 22-32.

Wohlman, B. B., (1973) Dictionary of Behavioral Science, compiled and edited by Benjamin Wohlman. Van Nostrand Reinhold, Co. New York.

Zajonc, R. B., (1980). Feeling and thinking: Preferences need no inferences. *American Psychologist.* 35, 151-175.

Zuckerman, M., Klorman, R., Larrance, D. T., & Spiegel, N. H.

(1981). Facial, Autonomic, and Subjective Components of Emotion: The Facial Feedback Hypothesis Versus the Externalizer-Internalizer Distinction. *Journal of Personality and Social Psychology,* 41(5), 929-944.

www.ingramcontent.com/pod-product-compliance
Lightning Source LLC
Chambersburg PA
CBHW051252050326
40689CB00007B/1160